On The Science of Changing Sex

A Layman's Guide to Transsexuality and Transgenderism

Kay Brown

DEDICATION

Thanks Jeff for always being there for me.

This book is dedicated to the memory of Kiira Trea who originally cajoled me into writing about this topic.

CONTENTS

1 INTRODUCTION

Although I had been taken to therapists since I was ten years old, I was first seen by the Stanford Gender Dysphoria Clinic, when I was 17 years old, taken by my parents, in the mid-70s, in the middle of my senior year in high school. I had been presenting as a girl part-time in high-school, or rather, after school hours, to go shopping with my female friends and flirt with boys. I transitioned full time right after graduation. Although to say that I "transitioned" is misleading. It was more like I stopped presenting as a boy, as I had no more need to do so.

At the age of 18, I met other transsexuals for the first time, at the clinic. What I found surprised and confused me. They did not seem to be unaffectedly feminine, without effort, but more like very masculine men who desired to be feminine and were working desperately to appear so. It was early on Saturday morning but a fair number were wearing out of fashion cocktail and party dresses and way too much make-up. I was acutely embarrassed for them. Most were much older. Many of them had been, or still were, happily and sexually satisfactorily married to women for years. I couldn't understand why they wanted to live as women.

If I was surprised and confused by them, they were just as surprised and confused by me. I had dated straight boys who had been high school classmates, besides the young men that I met when I left home. None of the others at the Clinic had ever dated a man nor seemed at all interested in doing so.

During a break, several transwomen, all much older, crowded, towering around and over me, making me very uncomfortable as they alternately commented on my looks, my age, even my body, in an obviously lascivious and simultaneously jealous way. One of them asked about my romantic life. I replied that I was dating some young men. One asked,

"How is that possible?!?"

"They ask me out; I say yes," I shrugged.

After that, I found a crowd of kids my own age, not associated with the clinic, all of whom were like me. They looked, sounded, and acted like girls. Also like me, they were dating men. Most of them were very socially and financially disenfranchised; while I was the product of a privileged upper-middle-class family living in an affluent suburban neighborhood, I was then intermittently homeless due to being effectively disowned by my family. I had some adjustments to make in my preconceptions and values. But like shipwrecked sailors, all in the same lifeboat, we were "sisters". It was from these kids that I really learned what I needed to know to survive as a transsexual, living as a young woman. We pal'ed around, went dancing with men at straight night clubs together for mutual support, helped each other with hair and make-up before big dates, and talked endlessly together about men.

We also talked about transsexuals. We talked about how the older ones seemed to be quite different than us. One comment that I heard was, "They are just TVs (transvestites) that need a bigger fix".

"Transsexual", one word for two very different types of people. I knew this with a vague awareness. This did not bother me. And, I thought that others knew and understood that there were the two different types. Didn't we all talk and write about the differences between "early transitioning" and "late transitioning" types?

But the public and even many in the so called "Transgender Community" don't know the full story. Some deliberately suppress that knowledge and/or spread misinformation. Why do they do this? The Transkids.us FAQ explained it best,

> *"… the most socially and economically advantaged sector of the transsexual population consisted of autogynephilic transsexuals and they found it psychologically and culturally advantageous to embrace an articulation of autogynephilia in terms of a concept of "gender identity" which maintained that one could have an internalized and hidden feminine "gender" while simultaneously living a seemingly normal social and sexual life as a man. Pragmatically, it was expedient to erase the distinctions between types of transsexuals. … given that the "transgender" community is controlled entirely by autogynephilic transsexuals who have a vested interest in this "gender identity." model and the medical community of surgeons, endocrinologists, and gender therapists, is now tailor built around their needs, both are resistant to*

any acknowledgement of the {two type taxonomy} or the acknowledgement of homosexual transsexuality as a separate condition. If {this} understanding of autogynephilia were accepted, it would undermine the "transgendered" community's construction of gender identity which they view as a route to legitimacy and acceptance. If {homosexual transsexuals) were acknowledged {as a separate group} it would be even more damaging because it would reveal inconsistencies in autogynephilic {transwomens'} personal narratives and the understanding of their own condition. Since their political and social identity is built around the notion that they were always really "female" because they "feel like women on the inside", that transkids who present far more cross gender attributes pre-transition, and are more convincing as women post-transition, do not share their unique psychology, would undermine the credibility of the way they think about their own disorder."

Because of this conflation of two very different groups of people with very different needs, the medical, social, and legal needs of homosexual transsexuals, including transkids, are short-changed. This book seeks to correct that.

Remember as you read this book; Transsexuals people are good people, worthy of our respect, and even of our admiration. Nothing in this material is meant to imply otherwise. If you are a transsexual: You have value as a human being. You have the right to be respected, valued, and even celebrated as the gender to which you identify and aspire regardless of etiology.

This book is written for the lay reader. I have deliberately avoided the academic practice of including distracting in-line citation references, footnotes, and chapter endnotes. Those sexologists who would welcome them likely already know the references and for those lay readers who wish to cross-check my assertions, I provide the references and much more in a bibliography at the end, organized by topic. I've also avoided providing tables of statistics, charts, and graphs as I've noted that my blog essays that include and explain them are the least popular. However, I do list two simple to use statistical numbers that represent the relative difference between populations, Cohen's d and Mahalanobis' D. One doesn't need to know the technical details to understand them: The bigger the number, the bigger the difference.

2 BRAIN SEX AND BEHAVIOR

Before one explores the nature of transsexuality, one first has to cover the nature of non-transsexuality, men and women, heterosexual and homosexual, and the differences between them, specifically the sexually dimorphic brain and the behavioral differences that are likely to arise from it.

Your brain is like a muscle: Use it or lose it… and it responds to sex hormones, which are really "growth hormones", but with specific areas of the body that are targets for sexually dimorphic development.

In exploring the possibility that transsexuals may have a "brain sex" that is similar to their preferred gender identity, we are also stepping into the realm of gender politics in general. What is the difference between men and women? Is there a significant difference between them? Once upon a time, in pre-feminist days, the early 19th Century, scientists supported the then prevailing view that women's' minds were inferior to men. Proof of such was found in the measurable fact that women have, on average, smaller brains than men. Of course, women also, on average, are both shorter and weigh less, so really, was this difference in brain size a significant one? Then, came a more unbiased age (relatively speaking) in which it was shown that women and men have similar mental abilities, similar intelligence, and most importantly, similar potential for intellectual achievement. Thus, came an age where to suggest that men's and women's brains might differ in significant ways, was academically unpopular. But nagging differences were still found… in animals.

In animal research, one could side step sexual politics, as well as ethical problems of experimenting on humans. In animals, in the early to mid-20th Century, it was found that sex hormones, were responsible for brain changes during critical periods in development which led to sexually dimorphic behaviors in adulthood, especially those related to sexual behavior, sexual preference, and rearing of young. One could castrate a young male rat and that rat would fail to behave in the typical masculine fashion as an adult. Similarly, one could inject a young female rat with testosterone, and that female rat would later mount other female rats as an adult. Dissection of these rats showed that certain regions of their brains showed sexually dimorphic structures that were changed to be more like the opposite sex to the presence or lack of testosterone. Since these behaviors are similar in nature to behaviors found in humans this led to the belief that these changes should be present in human brains as well, and that humans should have sexually dimorphic brain structures as well. In the beginning of the research into possible sexually dimorphic brain structures, it was thought that there were only a few areas involved. But, as techniques for brain research improved, it was found that more and more areas were involved. Eventually, it became standard practice to consider each part of the brain sexually dimorphic until proven otherwise!

From the early work, it was recognized that some areas of the brain must be sexually dimorphic from early in embryonic development, while others only become sexually dimorphic later. It has been found that some effects are 'locked-in' by exposure to sex hormones at different times in development. There are associated behavioral consequences to these locked in changes. These are referred to as "organizational effects" of the sex hormones. Other effects were found to occur later, and even be reversible, for example, testosterone will increase both libido and aggressive behaviors, and even improve one's spatial navigation and mental object rotation skills, while estrogen will increase verbal language skills. But, stop taking these hormones, and the effects will reverse back to previous levels. These kinds of effects are called "activation effects". Both of these kinds of effects involve changes in both relative size, morphology, and density of neural connections in different areas of the brain. It turns out, that using cross-sex hormones, even in adulthood, really does make one's brain look more like the other sex!

Recently, it has been found that some sexually dimorphic features of the brain are associated with differentially expressed genes found on the sex chromosomes. The extent to which this is automatic simply due to one's karyotype or mediated by sex hormones is not yet known.

Just how sexually dimorphic is the human brain?

Before recent developments in neuroimaging, most scientists would have said that there was no way that we could determine the sex / gender of a person looking only at their brain. In fact, I DID say exactly that. But now, that is not an accurate statement, at least not wholly accurate, because a recent paper/letter has shown that with increased resolution and computer power we can determine the sex of a person that a particular brain resides in, just from an analysis of the 3D MRI image of their brains to 93% accuracy. The mere fact that this can be done shows that the human brain is in fact highly sexually dimorphic, because if we were to simply guess, we would only be right 50% of the time.

The number, 93%, sounded suspiciously familiar. That's about the number of people who are not LGBT in the population. Given that we also know that LGB people are likely to have sexually dimorphic features that as a population, are shifted towards that of the opposite sex, we can propose an hypothesis and a prediction. If this analysis were redone excluding all known LGBT people, that the mathematical regression would result in greater predictive strength. It would not reach 100% because there would still be those who due to social desirability bias would fail to accurately disclose their sexual orientation and thus still be included in the heterosexual study group. Increasing the accuracy in that instance will add evidence to a quip that I have made before, that humans don't have male and female brains so much as androphilic and gynephilic brains.

There's an important point that is missed by people discussing the issue of whether the human brain is sexually dimorphic or not; The size and shape of any specific feature of the brain is to an extent only a very crude estimate of the number of neurons and the connection density of that region. It does not tell us the functional differences, if any, that that difference represents. As Cordelia Fine has pointed out, these differences, though they clearly exist, does not tell us what, if any, the differences may be in men's and women's **minds**. Only additional research will help us determine these.

But still, anyone who still says that it is not possible to determine the sex of a human brain by looking at it (with the right tools) hasn't been keeping up with the science.

If one were to "guess" the sex of the brain to 93% accuracy means that the effect size (Cohen's d) would, if it were a single dimorphic feature, be a whopping 3.0 !!!! That's an over the top value. Thus, as we get better imaging tools to see the fine details, we are learning that the human brain, in terms of multivariate statistics of multiple measurements at all points of the brain, is in fact extremely sexually dimorphic. The problem is that no one area is all that dimorphic, but in aggregate, they are quite dimorphic. That is to say, if one area is slightly dimorphic, giving a small statistical clue as to the sex of the individual, and a second area is also slightly dimorphic, giving a small clue as the sex of the individual, the two can be used together to give a medium sized clue to increase the accuracy… and with many, many, areas, each additively pointing towards one sex or the other, the accuracy gets quite good.

Given that brains and minds are intimately linked, that minds are the function of brains, the fact that both brain mosaic features and personality traits are both individually only mildly sexually dimorphic, but collectively very dimorphic should not surprise us.

The idea that men and women have different personalities has been widely accepted for millennia, but recently has been seriously questioned by feminists and some social scientists and psychologists, most notably Prof. Janet S. Hyde. But even she, in propounding the "Gender Similarity Hypothesis" did find obviously sexually dimorphic behaviors in humans, as Guidice, et al remarked,

> *"Specifically, Hyde found consistently "large" (d between .66 and .99) or "very large" (d≥1.00) sex differences in only some motor behaviors and some aspects of sexuality; "moderate" differences (d between .35 and .65) in aggression"*

"…some aspects of sexuality…" As in sexual orientation, the single largest sexually dimorphic difference between men and women (d=5.9), also motor behaviors that are highly correlated with sexual orientation. Finally, aggression; yes, men are more aggressive than women by nature. But what of the more subtle areas of personality?

In this study by Guidice, the authors chose to use a very well established personality inventory, the 16PF which underlie the more well-known Big Five factor personality inventory.

First, we need to discuss the matter of looking at individual aspects of personality as single variables then averaging this difference between the sexes as the authors pointed out,

> *"The problem with this approach is that it fails to provide an accurate estimate of overall sex differences; in fact, average effect sizes grossly underestimate the true extent to which the sexes differ. When two groups differ on more than one variable, many comparatively small differences may add up to a large overall effect; in addition, the pattern of correlations between variables can substantially affect the end result. As a simple illustrative example, consider two fictional towns, Lowtown and Hightown. The distance between the two towns can be measured on three (orthogonal) dimensions:*

longitude, latitude, and altitude. Hightown is 3,000 feet higher than Lowtown, and they are located 3 miles apart in the north-south direction and 3 miles apart in the east-west direction. What is the overall distance between Hightown and Lowtown? The average of the three measures is 2.2 miles, but it is easy to see that this is the wrong answer. The actual distance is the Euclidean distance, i.e., 4.3 miles — almost twice the "average" value. The same reasoning applies to between-group differences in multidimensional constructs such as personality. When groups differ along many variables at once, the overall between-group difference is not accurately represented by the average of univariate effect sizes; in order to properly aggregate differences across variables while keeping correlation patterns into account, it is necessary to compute a multivariate effect size. The Mahalanobis distance D is the natural metric for such comparisons. Mahalanobis' D is the multivariate generalization of Cohen's d, and has the same substantive meaning. Specifically, D represents the standardized difference between two groups along the discriminant axis; for example, $D = 1.00$ means that the two group centroids are one standard deviation apart on the discriminant axis."

Using Mahalonobis' D allows us to see the real difference in personalities of men and women taking into account the global pattern of multiple personality traits, rather than one at a time. From this the authors found,

"We found a global effect size $D = 2.71$, corresponding to an overlap of only 10% between the male and female distributions. Even excluding the factor showing the largest univariate ES, the global effect size was $D = 1.71$ (24% overlap). These are extremely large differences by psychological standards. The idea that there are only minor differences between the personality profiles of males and females should be rejected as based on inadequate methodology."

That 10% overlap sounds awfully familiar — That's similar to that found for the global pattern of the sexually dimorphic mosaic of the brain. And just as I suggested that this might represent the effect of the non-heterosexual population, again we can hypothesize that we might see a larger effect size if all known LGBT folk were excluded from the study subjects. If so, that would further support the hypothesis that humans don't have sexually dimorphic brains so much as having androphilic vs. gynephilic ones.

Guidice did a replication of this study using larger data set which, as the authors put it,

"Our results corroborate the original study (with a comparable if somewhat smaller effect size)..."

Their effect size in the replication study was still very large at D=2.10.

We have solid, reproducible, evidence that men and women are quite sexually dimorphic in both brain morphology and some behaviors.

But here is where a note of caution must be interjected. The vast range of human behaviors also include many, in fact most, behaviors that are NOT sexually dimorphic. For example, most high level cognitive functions are NOT sexually dimorphic. In spite of persistent sexist stereotypes, men are NOT better at math, science, computer programming, or abstract thinking than women. The full list is too long to enumerate here.

3 GENDER ATYPICALITY AND SEXUAL ORIENTATION

I've deliberately avoided using the popular term "gender non-conforming", using the term "gender atypical" instead. It may have struck some of my readers as odd and idiosyncratic, given that so many others use the "GNC" term. But, I have done so for several important reasons, some based on science, some on political-philosophical grounds.

The scientific reasons are easier to explain. There is no "standard" to which behavior should "conform". There is only behavior, period. However, if we look at, study in depth as scientists, a species we can say that there are behaviors that are far more commonly performed by them than other behaviors seen in other species. These we can label as "typical" for that species. If we see a behavior in a given individual of a species that is uncommon for that species, we may label it "atypical"; but we would never label it "non-conforming" since we can't really say what standard that a given species should "conform" to. Behaviors are selected by evolution depending upon whether they increase the reproductive 'fitness' of the individuals exhibiting them. The same logic applies to sexes within a given species. We may observe sexually dimorphic behaviors in a given species. That is, we will label a behavior sexually dimorphic if we see that it is much more commonly performed in one sex than the other. If we see an individual performing such a behavior that is uncommon in that given sex, we may label it "atypical" for that sex; but to label it "non-conforming"? That's smacks of invoking an outside agency which has the authority to define a standard for such behavior that the theory of natural selection does not provide. Just as with non-human species, humans do not stand outside of nature. There is no agency that defines for our species a standard by which to judge whether a given behavior does or does not "conform".

The political reasons include my personal objection to the very notion that there should be such a "standard". But even deeper, is my objection to the post-modernist idea that there are no intrinsic sexually dimorphic behaviors in humans, that there are only socially constructed roles. This notion would state that since all differences in behavior observed between the human sexes are socially constructed and maintained, there must be a socially defined standard to which we can conform or not. Another idea that I object to is that of a divinely ordained standard that we must conform to, which has the same effect. Thus, both of these ideas reduce any behavior that is seen in an individual that is uncommon in that person's sex to an act of "gender non-conformity" either by accident or by will... but never by nature. I find both the notion that we stand outside of nature to be scientifically preposterous and philosophically silly.

To say that a given behavior is masculine or feminine is to say that that behavior is more likely to be produced by one sex than the other, this is, it denotes that the behavior is both sexually dimorphic and in which sex it is more commonly found. For example, in common rabbits, a female is far more likely to pull hair from its belly to line an underground nest in preparation for caring for kits (newborn rabbits). Thus, in rabbits, nest lining would be a "feminine" behavior. In rodents, females are far more likely than males to exhibit lordosis, arching of the spine to tilt and raise the pelvis, than males, usually in the presence of an adult male. So we can describe lordosis as also being "feminine" behavior. Conversely, mounting behavior is usually only seen in males, and thus may be described as a "masculine" trait.

In humans, there are a range of behaviors that show varying levels of sexual dimorphism. Simple observation would suggest that the single most sexually dimorphic trait in humans is the propensity for sexual attraction to men. In women, approximately 98% exhibit sexual attraction to men, while in men perhaps only 5-10% are attracted to other men, and only 3% are exclusively so. Thus, sexual attraction to men would, by our definition, be a "feminine" trait. Interestingly, there appears to be analogs to "mounting behavior" and "lordosis" in humans. Men who are sexually attracted to other men, also exhibit a preference for mounting (active or "top") or lordosis (passive or "bottom"). It is my thesis here that in gay men, independent sexually dimorphic behaviors have been feminized while others have not, and that this independent switching has occurred in varying combinations in individual men. That is to say, that a gay man could be quite feminized in at least one behavior (androphilia) but show a range of other behaviors that may or may not also be feminine and thus, gender atypical to varying degrees.

It's important to differentiate between behaviors that are demonstrably sexually dimorphic because of neural correlates and those that are merely cultural role enactments and false gender stereotypes. We should also differentiate between a strong social construction hypothesis which says that all differences in behavior are purely from culture and a weak social construction hypothesis that says that some behaviors and gender roles are socially constructed around truly sexually dimorphic behaviors and gender role limitations built around cultural prejudice and false stereotypes. The weak social construction hypothesis is easily defended and has much evidence to support it. For example, it is fairly obvious that different clothing fashion for men and women is socially constructed (though influenced by somatic sexual dimorphism). It is the strong social construction hypothesis that is not supported by the evidence.

Earlier I made reference to the single most sexually dimorphic behavior in humans: androphilia (sexual attraction to adult males). In female humans, it is extremely common to be attracted to men. One could object to this being a 'natural' phenomena and say that social expectations have defined this. But it would not fit the evidence that has been amassing that sexual orientation is neither "chosen" nor "taught". Further, why should humans be unique in the world? Most mammalian species are sexually dimorphic in their sexual attractions. (No, I'm not denying that same sex behavior occurs in non-human species… only saying it is not as common as other sex attraction.) But, this isn't the end of the story.

Sexual orientation in adults is presaged by gendered behavior as young children. That is to say, that humans have sexually dimorphic behaviors as young children and that sexual orientation is highly correlated with those behaviors. Children that grow up to be homosexual evince notable gender atypicality. The key behaviors that are noted to be gender atypical in boys are avoidance of rough and tumble play, avoidance of physical aggression, and preference for female playmates and play style, etc. There are also more subtle, less easily measured, but still quite real sexually dimorphic behaviors that correlate with sexual orientation more than they do with sex per se, such as motor movements, vocal production, etc. But here is where we start to see the issue of having to contend with those prejudices. Some cultures attach serious negative stigma to gender atypicality and non-heterosexuality while others do not.

4 NATURE VS. NURTURE

Given the ongoing "culture war" regarding sexual orientation, wherein some elements of society wish to portray homosexuality as "sinful", "mental illness", or both it is no surprise that the question of etiology of homosexuality, and indeed of any sexual orientation, has become a political, as well as scientific question. Into this fray has come some of the best and brightest of the sexologists who are exploring the science. I know that some transsexuals and transgendered folk won't like to read the name of the lead author, but in science, it is not important who says something, but what the evidence says. The lead author is J. Michael Bailey. Yes, that Prof. Bailey.

Bailey is joined by Lisa Diamond, Paul Vassey, Marc Breedlove, Eric Vilain, and Mark Epprecht in a masterful compilation and exposition on the current science of sexual orientation. The paper also covers evidence concerning androphilic MTF transgender people and covers some remarkable conjectures regarding the role of culture, nurture if you will, regarding the difference between MTF transkids and conventional gay men.

The paper lays out powerful evidence that shows that indeed "nature" has a very strong role to play in the development of sexual orientation. But as the authors point out, this does NOT mean that morally or politically such evidence, or indeed proof, has any bearing on how society should treat non-heterosexual people,

"Ongoing political controversies around the world exemplify a long-standing and widespread preoccupation with the acceptability of homosexuality. Nonheterosexual people have seen dramatic surges both in their rights and in positive public opinion in many Western countries. In

contrast, in much of Africa, the Middle East, the Caribbean, Oceania, and parts of Asia, homosexual behavior remains illegal and severely punishable, with some countries retaining the death penalty for it. Political controversies about sexual orientation have often overlapped with scientific controversies. That is, participants on both sides of the sociopolitical debates have tended to believe that scientific findings—and scientific truths—about sexual orientation matter a great deal in making political decisions. The most contentious scientific issues have concerned the causes of sexual orientation— that is, why are some people heterosexual, others bisexual, and others homosexual? The actual relevance of these issues to social, political, and ethical decisions is often poorly justified, however. ... No causal theory of sexual orientation has yet gained widespread support. The most scientifically plausible causal hypotheses are difficult to test. However, there is considerably more evidence supporting nonsocial causes of sexual orientation than social causes. This evidence includes the cross-culturally robust finding that adult homosexuality is strongly related to childhood gender nonconformity; moderate genetic influences demonstrated in well-sampled twin studies; the cross-culturally robust fraternal-birth-order effect on male sexual orientation; and the finding that when infant boys are surgically and socially "changed" into girls, their eventual sexual orientation is unchanged (i.e., they remain sexually attracted to females). In contrast, evidence for the most commonly hypothesized social causes of homosexuality—sexual recruitment by homosexual adults, patterns of disordered parenting, or the influence of homosexual parents—is generally weak in magnitude and distorted by numerous confounding factors.

Setting aside the issues of policy and etiology, there are still some important issues regarding cultural factors influencing expression of androphilia in males because one of the models of why non-heterosexual orientations may persist is that of kin selection, in which the gender atypicality of androphilic males is evolutionarily selected for and maintained in the population because androphilic males help their near relatives raise their children, thereby increasing the chances of their own genes, shared with those close relatives, to perpetuate. In this model, gender atypical androphilic males are in effect, an evolutionarily 'fit' alternative 'morph'; far from being a "mistake of nature", they are in a very real sense, a "third sex" involved in reproduction by proxy through childcare.

Consistent with the predictions of the Kin Selection Hypothesis (KSH), research conducted in Samoa on transgender androphilic males (fa'afafine) has repeatedly demonstrated that they show elevated avuncular (uncle-like) tendencies compared to Samoan women and gynephilic men. (This is measured via a 9-item scale measuring willingness to care for, and to give resources to, nieces and nephews. Furthermore, this finding does not appear to reflect a general tendency to help others, but a specific preference for kin. In contrast, research on cisgender androphilic males in Western populations and non-Western industrialized cultures has garnered virtually no support for the KSH. It is possible that elevated avuncularity is not expressed unless male androphilia takes on the transgender form. More research is needed to ascertain whether other populations of transgender male androphiles exhibit elevated kin-directed altruism or not. ... Societies in which transgender male androphilia predominates exhibit a significantly greater presence of human ancestral sociocultural conditions compared to societies in which the cisgender form predominates. This suggests that the transgender form of male androphilia was likely the ancestral form. As such, transgender male androphilia likely represents the best model for testing evolutionary hypotheses, given that more derived forms of this trait may reflect recent cultural/historical influences that might obscure the outcome of evolutionary processes. Consequently, the most promising results from tests of both the KSH and SAGH are from studies of Samoan fa'afafine. The evidence would be much stronger if other populations of transgender androphilic males showed similar effects."

Let's think about this a moment. If the so called Western form, conventional gay men, don't show an interest in their kin, is that because their homophobic siblings won't let them, or because trying to be gender typical (straight acting) includes disavowing any interests in what would be considered womanly interest in young children? Or could it be that there really is a difference between non-transsexual and transsexual androphilic males? I know it's only anecdotal, but my reader may wish to check out my own history of a very strong interest in children. Also note that my siblings have forbidden me from having anything to do with their children, due to extreme religious notions and transphobia.

(Note to researchers: Can we please use the more gender identity respectful term 'materteral' instead of 'avuncular', if we are speaking of transsexual MTF folk here?)

Here is where things get really interesting. The authors conjecture here that cultural factors influence the form that male androphilia takes depends upon the culture that androphilic males find themselves in,

"Same-sex sexuality between adults typically takes one of two cross-culturally recurrent forms, which are related to gender-role enactment and gender identity. These two forms are cisgender and transgender male androphilia and female gynephilia.

Cisgender male androphiles and female gynephiles occupy the gender role typical of their sex and identify as "men" and "women," respectively. This is

the form of homosexuality that is nearly universal in the contemporary West. In contrast, transgender male androphiles and female gynephiles do not occupy the gender role typical of their sex. Not only do they behave in a highly gender-atypical manner, but they often identify, and are identified by others, as neither "men" nor "women," but rather, as a member of some alternative gender category. Contemporary examples of transgender male androphiles include the kathoey of Thailand, the xanith of Oman, the muxes of Mexico, and the fa'afafine of Samoa. Some contemporary examples of transgender female gynephiles include the tombois of Sumatra and the mahu of Tahiti.

Cisgender male androphiles and female gynephiles behave in a relatively gender-typical manner when compared with their transgender counterparts. However, they are relatively gender-atypical when compared to gynephilic cisgender men and androphilic cisgender women. Thus, regardless of the form they take, male androphilia and female gynephilia are associated with gender-atypicality. However, the strength of this association varies with the manner in which same-sex sexuality is publicly expressed.

Both the cisgender and transgender forms of same-sex sexuality may occur within a given culture, but typically one or the other predominates. For example, the cisgender form tends to be much more common in many Western cultures. In contrast, the transgender form appears to be more common in many non-Western cultures. In places where the two forms coexist, their members often consider each other to be part of the same subculture. Margaret Mead observed a meeting in which an Omaha minquga (i.e., a transgender male androphile) and a Japanese homosexual man (i.e., a cisgender male androphile) who visited her field site in 1961 instantly recognized each other. Within an hour of the Japanese man's arrival, the sole minquga in the tribe turned up and tried to make contact with him. Similarly, sociologist Fredrick Whitam noted that, in São Paulo, travesti (transgender male androphiles) are an especially conspicuous presence in gay clubs and are treated with a high degree of respect.

In contemporary Western cultures, cisgender male androphiles typically engage in sexual interactions with each other; the same is true of cisgender female gynephiles. That is, in the West, homosexual relationships are typically between two homosexual individuals. Such individuals comprise the Western gay and lesbian communities. This type of same-sex sexual relationship has been referred to as "egalitarian" and is characterized by partners who are not markedly different in age or gender-related characteristics. Within such relationships, partners tend not to adopt special social roles, and they treat each other as equals. In contrast, this pattern appears to be relatively uncommon in non-Western cultures and has emerged only recently in certain non-Western urban centers.

> *Although transgender male androphiles are same-sex attracted, they rarely, if ever, engage in sexual activity with each other; the same is true of transgender female gynephiles. Rather, these individuals engage in sexual activity with same-sex cisgender partners who self-identify, and are identified by others, as "men" or "women." For example, in Samoa, very feminine natal males called fa'afafine (which means "in the manner of women") have sex with masculine Samoan men. The fa'afafine would be aghast at the idea of having sex with one another.*

> *Little research has focused on the cisgender sexual partners of same-sex-attracted transgender males and females. Blackwood noted that, in Sumatra, the cisgender female partners (femmes) of tombois "assert an uncomplicated attraction to men, [but] position themselves (if temporarily) under the label 'lesbi'"—a derivative of "lesbian." This suggests an episodic pattern of bisexual attraction on the part of femmes. In many cultures, same-sex sexual interactions between transgender and cisgender persons are not considered "homosexual" because they are understood to be hetero-gendered. In other words, if a cisgender androphilic male and a transgender androphilic male engage in sex, the former individual is often understood to be "the male partner" in the interaction, whereas the latter individual is often understood to be "the female partner." Accordingly, the interaction is understood as male-female rather than male-male."*

For the sake of a thought experiment, let us concede for the moment that the form that male androphilia takes depends on the culture that they find themselves. (This will not be a popular notion among neither Western Gay men nor autogynephiles who would otherwise wish to identify as androphilic transwomen.) Let us further assume that the Kinship Selection Hypothesis is correct. This would support not only the notion that androphilic males are a special morph, but that of necessity, the transgender form is the evolutionarily selected form. In which case, homosexual transsexuals are not "failed" or "self-hating" gay men as some mischaracterize them, but Western Gay Men are "failed" / "femmiphobic" transsexuals !!! This also reads upon efforts to "help" gender atypical children to be "more gender fluid", less gender atypical, less… well… less likely to be transsexual, is in fact an attempt to fight an evolutionarily selected and natural role, and as such is a "crime against nature".

However, what the authors didn't make clear is that every culture where homosexual transsexuals exist, there also exists side by side with them, the non-transsexual form, no exceptions. This does not mean that cultural factors don't have a role in how many there are of each, if in fact they are the same underlying taxon.

There is evidence that there may be more than one taxon of androphilic male, more than one etiology with different behavioral, and even physical, consequences. The key is one of the factors mentioned above, the Fraternal Birth Order Effect in which androphilic males are more likely to have older brothers than gynephilic males.

In learning about correlations between various behaviors and characteristics between exclusively androphilic transwomen and gay men, we may learn things that point to etiological factors that effect both. An interesting correlation is that in both gay men and androphilic transwomen, both populations exhibit the now famous Fraternal Birth Order Effect (FBOE) in which they have more older brothers than straight men. That is to say, that the more boys that a given mother gives birth to, the higher the chances of a boy being androphilic, either gay or transsexual. One of the chief hypothesis of the cause of the FBOE is the 'Maternal Immune Response' in which key proteins in male only development during a pregnancy enters the mother's bloodstream where the mother's immune system creates antibodies to fight off a mistaken "infectious agent": the male child. This in turn passes back to the male fetus where it interferes with normal male sexually dimorphic brain development, leading to a feminized brain. This effect can happen even to a first born child, but the FBOE would then come about because each male pregnancy increases the amount and strength of the immune response. Each male pregnancy increases the chances of the next male pregnancy resulting in an androphilic gender atypical male child, including the chance of a homosexual transsexual. The FBOE strongly supports a biological etiology for androphilia in males. But the effect seems to only explain a minority, estimated at 15% of androphilic males.

But the really interesting thing about this effect is that it is stronger for homosexual transsexuals than it is for gay men. This opens up some interesting avenues of research. Does this effect also mean that there is a correlation within the gay male population between measures of femininity and the FBOE? What about other characteristics that are more common in androphilic transwomen than in gay men?

The picture of homosexual transsexuality is that of early and notable gender atypical behavior, hypomasculine appearance (even before medical intervention) and near universal preference for anal receptive sexuality, "bottom" as it's called in the modern Western gay community, at least while still pre-op. Many gay men are just the opposite, preferring to "top" other gay men. So, is there are a correlation between preferred anal sex role and FBOE, childhood gender atypical behavior, or hypomasculine appearance? Are tops more like straight men in less FBOE, less gender atypicality, and more masculine appearance? Conversely, are bottoms more like transwomen?

In the Wienrich paper they found a correlation between childhood gender atypicality and a preference for being a bottom,

> *"The connections between childhood gender nonconformity (assessed by the Freund Feminine Gender Identity Scale, or FGI) and adult genitoerotic role (assessed by a sex history) were examined. ... Although other workers have cautioned against assuming a priori that childhood gender role is inherently related to adult preferences for particular sexual acts, our data suggest that there is at least a statistical association between these two concepts. In particular, the FGI (and many of its factors and items) are significantly associated with preferences for receptive anal intercourse and, less clearly, with oral-anal contact — but not with oral-genital intercourse or insertive anal intercourse. ... The data also suggest that in sex research involving homosexual men, the correct genitoerotic role distinction is not insertive vs. receptive behaviors, or even insertive vs. receptive anal intercourse, but receptive anal intercourse vs. all other behaviors."*

Thus, like transwomen, bottoms are more likely to have been gender atypical than tops.

In Moskowitz, they found that physical traits, relative masculinity, was correlated with sex role,

> *"We surveyed 429 men engaging in same-sex anal intercourse to investigate the degree to which anal penetrative self-identity was concordant with actual penetrative behavior. Additionally, the roles of masculinity and physical body traits (e.g., penis size, muscularity, height, hairiness, and weight) were tested as correlates of anal penetrative identity and identity-behavior concordance. ... Generally, tops reported larger penises than bottoms. They also reported being comparatively more masculine than bottoms. ... Our study suggests that the correlates of gay men's sexual self-labels may depend on objective traits in addition to the subjective pleasure associated with receptive or insertive anal intercourse."*

Thus, bottoms were more physically hypomasculine, just like homosexual transsexuals.

In the Wampold paper he explores the correlation between sex role and FBOE,

> *"Bottoms had a significantly greater mean number of older brothers than did Not-Bottoms. ... Thus, late fraternal birth order was correlated with receptive anal-erotic behavior among MSM."*

This same effect was found by Swift-Gallant,

> *"Only gay men with a bottom anal sex role showed evidence of a fraternal birth order effect. ... These results suggest that the fraternal birth order effect may apply to a subset of gay men who have a bottom anal sex role preference and that this subgroup is more gender-nonconforming."*

Thus, we've come full circle. There is evidence for a multivariate cluster of indicia in a subset of gay men that would appear to be very much like homosexual transsexuals save for one behavior, social transition to being transwomen. The question we then need to ask, is this difference between tops and bottoms dimensional or taxonic? It sure looks taxonic to me. The next question is the difference between bottom gay men and androphilic transwomen dimensional or taxonic? I'm betting it's dimensional.

The evidence thus suggests that there are (at least) two forms of androphilic males, only one of which includes homosexual transsexuals, while the other is the classic, "straight-looking / straight acting" gay man most associate with Western nations (though we have evidence that they also exist elsewhere).

If this is the case, what makes the difference between bottom gay men and homosexual transsexuals? We have strong hints that it is partially cultural and partially idiosyncratic. There are cultures where feminine androphilic males are granted greater latitude to express their native femininity and not be coerced into hiding in the closet, or attempting to pretend to be 'straight acting – straight looking' gay men like ours does. Assuming this to be the case, as our Western society is becoming less femmiphobic, transphobic, and misogynist, we should see more young gender atypical androphilic males persisting and choosing social transition as   transwomen.

5 TRANSSEXUAL VS. TRANSGENDER

The media and the press often talk and write as though "transgender" = "transsexual". That is to say, that there is an assumption that those who identify as transgender are all socially transitioning from one social sex to the other, prescribed cross-sex hormones, and either have or would strongly consider, if affordable, surgical interventions. Nothing could be further from the truth, as the vast, in fact, a super-majority, of such self-identified "transgender" people have not, nor do they wish to, permanently socially transition, nor are they gender dysphoric.

The word "transgender" was originally coined and used by Dr. Virginia Prince, a full time, lifestyle, autogynephilic cross-dresser, in the early '70s, to denote those like her/him as opposed to "transsexuals" who took hormones and had "sex change" surgery and also opposed to secretive "transvestites" who only occasionally cross-dressed, usually in private. Prince notoriously campaigned against autogynephiles choosing medical feminization, extolling the virtues of endogenous androgens. The term was meant to be exclusive of any other group, like drag artists or gender atypical gays or lesbians AND transsexuals.

But…

In the early '90s, Beth Elliott, using her nom de plume Mustang Sally, wrote an essay entitled, *"The Incredible Shrinking Identity"* in which she decried the social effects of subsuming transsexual people into the larger umbrella of "transgender", which with each passing year seemed to be growing at its margins to include more and more people who just a few years before, would never have been considered to be in the same grouping. Of course, she was mostly talking about secretive cross-dressers, "transvestites", autogynephilic men, who as we know, are in fact in the same etiological taxon as autogynephilic MTF transsexuals.

This has now become a serious scientific and civil rights issue as the term "transgender" has been stretched to the point where it has little meaning as to actual sexual, social, or gendered behavior. It is no longer enough for scientists to differentiate between autogynephilic/late onset vs. androphilic/early onset MTF transwomen… nor even between autoandrophilic vs. androphilic FtM transmen… now we must differentiate between an ever growing host of self-defined "other" gender categories and underlying behaviors, identities that are lumped under "transgender" to the point of making the term meaningless to sexologists and social scientists alike.

Flashback, 1980: Hanging out in the L.A. transsexual community, as it gained a political self-awareness, was a teenager; let's call her "Lee". Lee would tell anyone who asked that she was "transsexual"… yet caused great confusion to all who met her. She was natal female, short even for a woman, pleasantly plump, and decidedly feminine in both appearance and manner. She was in no sense gender atypical. And during the time that I knew her, over 18 months, she never made any attempt to present as a man, nor even as butch. She was always on the femmie side of androgynous to the point of being decidedly "cute" as she hung out, mostly with younger MTF transwomen whom she seemed to admire. Had she been hanging out in this same manner in the gay male scene, they would have likely labeled her a "Fag Hag". The transsexual community, while leery of non-trans males who would have acted this way, affectionately accepted Lee's non-threatening presence, while secretly rolling their eyes when she declared that she was "FtM".

Thinking back on Lee, I'm fairly certain that she never transitioned and I'm willing to place fairly high odds that she married and had kids, probably now has grandchildren, none of which have any idea that she once hung out in the trans-scene. At the time, we had no label for her. Today, on the internet, the FtM transsexual community does have a label that would have applied, "tucute", as in "Too Cute" to be transsexual. If you visit the FtM pages on Tumblr, you are sure to run into a few… and will also note that they in turn, grumble about the negative feedback they get from those they call "Truscum" ("true" masculine gynephilic FtM transsexuals) for not accepting that they too are just as "trans"; even if they are in no sense gender atypical nor gender dysphoric.

Recent Events: A few years ago, via her facebook page, a very socially liberal, rather prominent (and wealthy) venture capitalist in my professional circle proudly announced that her teenaged child was "transgender". I've been living "mostly stealth" in that most of my professional contacts do not know of my medical history (yes, I "pass"). But in a move to be supportive and perhaps even help her with the emotional issues that almost always come with a child's transition I came out to her. BAD MOVE! Nope, upon learning more about her child, it became very clear that her daughter had always been very gender typical as a girl, was not the least bit gender dysphoric, and had no intention of legally, socially, nor medically transitioning. No, she just wanted to be recognized as "transgender" and have everyone around her use gender neutral pronouns (cause ~~she is~~ they are so special, ~~she~~ they deserves it). There is another couple names for this behavior, "TransTrender" and "TrendsGender", as in it is now "trendy" to say that one is transgender, in the right circles. Back in my college years, hanging around Stanford University, I would often hear complaints from actual gynephilic women, real lesbians, about the phenomena of primarily androphilic women taking social positions as "Political Lesbians" and "Lesbians Until Graduation". The "transgender" community now has the same phenomena. It seems to have become "cool" in some comfortably well off, very socially liberal teenaged and young adult circles to be associated with the LGB and now T community, as though being associated with a marginalized group made up for their obvious social privilege.

One could well imagine the growing resentment felt by those who have experienced familial rejection, social disapprobation, economic deprivation, and psychic pain from a lifetime of gender atypicality and dysphoria towards those who misappropriate an identity from the protective cocoon of indulgent family, liberal universities, and the anonymity of the internet.

As one young transman ranting on tumblr put it,

> *"Dysphoria is the defining factor of a transgender person. It's why they want to TRANSition. It's why they're called TRANS in the first place, fuckwits. It doesn't have to be crippling "I hate my body ugh I can't look at myself naked" (And I do know some trans people whose dysphoria is that bad). On a 10 is an "I can't see myself naked" to 1 is a "I don't feel right in this body", I'm probably a 5-7. I can see myself naked but it just doesn't feel right. Specially with my chest. That's dysphoria. Not "omg I don't want to be human I want to be a rabbit/sunflower/magical girl" or whatever these tucutes are on I don't even know. ...*

> *The more I look at it, the more I see tucutes acting like being transgender is a cute little accessory they can put on. You're comfy with your body but you like girls even if you're a girl yourself? Congratulations, you could be a lesbian. You like boys but you're a boy? Good on you, you might be a homosexual man. You like the opposite gender? That makes you a terrible hetero person and that's bad because all hetero people are transphobic and evil. Be trans instead. That's cooler.*

Except… it's not.

It's not cool to be trans. It's not cool to wake up and see these parts of you that you feel so uncomfortable with having that you would wish cancer on yourself just to have them taken away. It's not cool to have to struggle with the longing to tell your parents that you're not the right gender because you want to trust them and want to open up to them but you're afraid it'll just add to the laundry list of things you've already disappointed them with. It's not cool to have known you were one thing from birth but everyone else and your own body telling you you're not and that you were supposed to be a certain way because that's what you looked like from the outside.

It's not cool to be trans.

If I had a choice, if being trans WAS a choice I would choose to be cis [non-transsexual]."

If these issues had stayed on the pages of tumblr and facebook, it wouldn't be a problem for science or those seeking better civil rights for transitioning transsexuals. But it hasn't. Consider a recent paper published in the *Journal of Youth and Adolescence* by Warnick et al. in which the authors very laudably explore the issues of safety and bathroom access for "transgender" youth. Ah… you are probably anticipating some of the problems that this might entail and you would be right. But let's explore each of them carefully.

In designing the study, the authors depended upon and cited the now popular William's estimate of 0.7% of the population in the US as "transgender". The problem with that study is that is the number who identify as "transgender" because William's did not apply any operational definition beyond asking if they were "transgender". Yet we know that only 0.03% of the U.S. population has actually socially transitioned, according to US Census study that cross-correlated with name/sex status changes to Social Security cards (arguably the absolute best estimate we will ever get to the number of individuals who actually transitioned). This means that less than 5% of those who identify as "transgender" ever transition. Thus, by definition, more than 95% of those who identify as "transgender" never transition, that in fact, they aren't all that gender dysphoric. So who are they?

How badly off are the numbers? In the Warnick study they found 86 individuals who self-identified as transgendered out of 935 students. Seriously, 9%? NINE &^%$#@ percent?!? That's more than three hundred times the number who actually transition. That's higher than the number of teens who grow up to be gay or lesbian. If the schools were statistically representative of the population as a whole, with only a thousand or so students, we could only expect a one in three chance of finding an actual transsexual among them, most likely an autogynephile who will transition as an adult and only one in fifteen chance of finding a transkid.

The design of this study was flawed from inception, as the numbers surveyed were never enough to find any statistically valid number of transkids, while using self-report of being "transgendered" without a valid operational definition lead only to a measure of the trendiness of the label in the teenaged population combined with "mischievous responders", kids saying 'shit' to mess with the study.

This problem has not gone completely unnoticed in the scientific literature. In a 2016 paper exploring this very issue, spelling it out in the title, "Prevalence of Transgender Depends on the "Case" Definition", paraphrasing their results,

> *"27 studies provided necessary data for a meta-analysis to evaluate the epidemiology of transgender and examine how various definitions of transgender affect prevalence estimates and to compare findings across studies that used different methodologies, in different countries, and over different periods. Overall estimates per 100,000 population were 9.2 for surgical or hormonal gender affirmation therapy and 6.8 for transgender-related diagnoses. Of studies assessing self-reported transgender identity, the estimate was 871; however, this result was influenced by a single outlier study. After removal of that study, the estimate changed to 355."*

These numbers tally very well with those from another study using US Census and Social Security data in which name and sex were changed in various US states. In that study no state had more than ~10 per hundred thousand. Note that this study was not included in the meta-analysis conducted by Collins, et al.

These numbers also tally with the several order of magnitude larger Williams estimate of those who self-identify as "transgender".

One of the most enlightening results of the Collins study was that though there was a slight increase in the number of actual gender dysphoric cases in a given clinic over time, there was no increase in prevalence over all, as clinics come and go. That is to say, there is no "epidemic" of gender dysphoria, there is only a vast increase in the number who publically self-identify as "transgender". As a quick guide for my reader, most males who self-identify as "transgender" are autogynephilic transvestites, erotically motivated private cross-dressers. Most females who self-identify as transgender (but are not gender dysphoric) are simply seeking to belong to an affinity group, to be in the "cool kids club".

Given the large disparities in the numbers, without an operational definition of "transgender" or "transsexual", a given study is almost assured to be about non-gender-dysphoric people.

Since we can't demand that people who self-identify as transgender stop doing so, this book uses the term, "transsexual". Only those who permanently social transition with some medical interventions are so designated.

6 THE TWO TYPES OF TRANSSEXUALS

There are two basic biological taxons (types) with their own unique etiologies (causes / conditions) that are found in transsexuals / transgendered people. They are mutually exclusive and distinct. That is to say, one and only one of these two conditions can be found in any one person, there is no overlap or blending between them. The conditions, and those people with them, only superficially resemble each other but are often confused and conflated with each other in the media, by the general public, and even by transsexuals and transgendered people themselves. That is to say, that there are two, and only two, separate "transgender spectrums".

But first, we need to define what is meant by taxonic, and what is not taxonic. As Gangestad explains it,

> *"Meehl defined a taxon as "a nonarbitrary class whose existence is conjectured as an empirical question, not a mere semantic convenience". A domain containing taxa is taxonic. Examples include biological sex, biological species, some disease entities (e.g., measles), and some ideological systems in politics or religion (Meehl, 1992). Many taxa are characterized by their causal simplicity. Taxonic domains are more likely than dimensional ones to have specific etiologies, including dichotomous necessary causal factors. For example, infectious diseases are taxa, and their causes consist of specific microbes. (More complex causal processes, such as thresholds and polarization effects, "may also underlie taxa".) The existence of taxa can be supported either by the demonstration of requisite causal processes or by formal mathematical taxometric methods, which decide whether latent taxa underlie a set of candidate indicators of a conjectured taxon based on numerical relations between them. If so, the formal-numerical taxa that are thereby defined are empirical. Their causal basis must be discovered through*

additional research, and, thereby, taxometric findings can guide future inquiry into the causes of variation in the domain.”

This is NOT like thinking of the two types as being the difference between a Pekinese and a Great Dane. The difference between these is "dimensional". Yes, they are different, but they are still the same species, both dogs... and dogs come in many sizes and shapes, but still all dogs.

Think of these two types of transsexuals as being separate species, perhaps like dogs and cats. They both run on four legs, are covered in fur, have the same number of claws, prefer to eat meat, make good pets, love being petted, both deserve to be treated well, etc. Yet, for all of their similarities, they are NOT the same animal. And while a Pekinese is the same size as a house cat, you wouldn't confuse the two.

Think: Laverne Cox vs. Caitlyn Jenner.

Think: Pose vs. TransParent.

Just as with cats and dogs, both types of transsexual people deserve to be treated well; both equally deserve legal, social, and medical recognition as the gender to which they identify and aspire.

One, often thought of as the "classic" pattern, the one that is most familiar in the public understanding, is extremely gender atypical from early childhood, often gender dysphoric from preschool age onward, and universally and exclusively attracted to their same natal sex (opposite of their gender identity) when they reach their teens and beyond. They have unstudied mannerisms and social behavior that more closely hews to those found in the other sex. They find their sexed body deeply repugnant and embarrassing from an early age, but increasingly so at puberty. Their cross-sex gender identity and decision to transition come early in life and feels like an easy and natural extension of their previous history. Unlike the other type, they do not experience sexual arousal with cross-dressing or to the thought of being or becoming the opposite sex.

Transsexuals with this etiology are most often called, "early onset" or "homosexual transsexuals" (HSTS) in the scientific literature. (This does not imply that they act like, nor identify, as gay or lesbian. It only means that they are sexually and affectionally attracted to gender typical members of the same natal sex. This term is very often considered offensive by the very people it describes and should only be used in scientific papers and discussions, if at all.) As children and teens they are sometimes called "transgender children", "transkids", or "transgendered youth" (transyouth) in common parlance.

There are some differences in life arcs of Female-to-Male (FtM) and

Male-To-Female (MTF) transkids. The median age of transition for MTF of this type is 20 years old, with a range of early puberty to mid-20's. More than 95% transition full time before the age of 25 and it is unheard of to find one who transitions full time after age 30. The median age of transition for FtMs is slightly older, with a moderate number transitioning in their 30's and later, usually after having attempted to live as very butch (masculine) lesbians. Thinking about transkids as individuals who are so like the opposite sex that they might as well be that sex offers a straight forward and insightful way of viewing these kids.

The other type of transsexual is generally gender typical in behavior as a child, adolescent, and into early adulthood, but may experience transient gender dysphoria, none the less, usually kept secret, due to shame. (Note: These children, teenagers, and adults are hiding their desire to be, or be like, the other sex, not gender atypical behavior, which they don't naturally have.) Their cross-gender identity takes time to develop and solidify as the process is often quite emotionally distressing, confusing, and vacillating. They are mostly attracted to the opposite natal sex and to other transgendered people, especially to early onset transsexuals (who universally are NOT interested in return), but may be behaviorally bisexual or asexual. They exhibit an unusual sexual arousal pattern, a particular sexual orientation, usually called an Erotic Target Location Error in the scientific literature, in which they map their preferred sexual object, the opposite sex, onto their own bodies and actions, and thus find the thought of being or becoming the opposite sex to be arousing and emotionally rewarding, leading to an Erotic Target Identity Inversion, in which they come to identify as a member of the class of people to which they are attracted, specifically, the opposite sex. They may also find altering their appearance to approximate the opposite sex, by cross-dressing, to also be sexually arousing and emotionally rewarding. In Female-to-Male (FtM) transgendered individuals, it is called "autoandrophilia" (AAP) and in Male-To-Female (MTF) transgendered individuals this arousal pattern is called "autogynephilia" (AGP). (When referring to both autoandrophilia and autogynephilia "A*P" may be used.) Transsexuals with this etiology are most often called, "non-homosexual transsexuals" or "late onset" in the scientific literature.

Before transition, the natural behavior of late-onset / non-homosexual / autogynephilic MTF transsexuals is gender typical, easily passing as typical straight men, often marrying women, fathering children, and successful in stereotypically masculine and even hyper-masculine (e.g. Navy Seal) careers. It is not uncommon for them to exhibit homophobic and sexist attitudes. As it can take years for the cross-gender identity to form and establish itself, the modal age for transition is 35 to 40 years old, the mean is between 40 to

45, with a range of early 20's to very old age. They are far more likely to transition in individualistic cultures than socially interdependent cultures. After transition, they may identify as lesbian, asexual/uncertain, bisexual, or even straight women, including marrying men. Thinking about autogynephilic MTF transsexuals as "male bodied people who love women and (romantically) want to become what they love" offers a more accurate and more richly informative way to understand them.

Before transition, the natural behavior of non-homosexual / autoandrophilic FtM may be quite variable, but is usually less "butch" than exclusively gynephilic FtM transsexuals. Their families would likely describe them as having been very typical girls, with some tomboyish interests, comfortable being feminine (dresses, make-up, nail polish, etc.). Their sexuality is most likely to be also variable over time, where they may find men or women more attractive as partners at different times in their lives. Overt erotic cross-dressing occurs only rarely, but other aspects of autoandrophilia may be found in their fantasy life (e.g. erotic interest in Yaoi Manga and/or M/M Alpha/Omega novels) or having crushes on FtM transkids. We know less about such transmen as we do autogynephilic transwomen, but that is changing rapidly.

Because of the difference in mean age at transition, the first type is often called, "early" or "young transitioner" and the second type "older" or "late transitioner" within the transsexual communities. However, the range of age at transition of the two types overlaps and this nomenclature may thus be misleading, especially for a "late transitioner" who transitions "early". It is important to remember that the key difference between the two is that the first type is exclusively, or primarily, "homosexual" with regard to natal sex and gender atypical in natural behavior and manner, making it difficult to fit in as their natal sex, while the second type is defined by their atypical sexuality, being aroused by the thought of being or becoming the opposite sex. Again, Think: Laverne Cox vs. Caitlyn Jenner.

It is important to understand that these are NOT different theoretical categories, but different names that focus on different aspects of the distinct differences between the two types (taxa). These terms all refer to the same two types. For example "Early Onset" refers to those whose gender atypicality and dysphoria are evident to observers as pre-adolescents while "Late Onset" refers to those whose gender dysphoria and associated behavior (cross-dressing, etc.) begin at or after adolescence.

This taxonomy is very well documented in Male-To-Female transsexuals, less so in Female-to-Males. They were first described over a hundred years ago by Magnus Hirschfeld in his book, *Transvestites*. Studies, going back to the 1970's, looking at the correlation between sexual orientation, age of transition, childhood gender atypicality, appearance, biodemographics, cross-cultural correlations, neuroanatomy, and autogynephilia consistently find two statistically significant groupings with very large effect sizes. Most importantly, evidence, based on predictions regarding the taxonomy, continue to support the two type taxonomy, especially in MTF transsexuals.

One group is primarily attracted to men, transitions quite young, passed as girls/women with relative ease, were noted to be feminine (sissy boys) by parents and teachers as children, preferred female playmates, avoided rough'n'tumble play, and were unlikely to report finding wearing women's clothing to be sexually arousing (less than 15% of self-identified androphilic MTF report erotic arousal to cross-dressing).

The other grouping was sexually attracted to women (as evidenced by extensive sexual experience with women, marriage, and siring children) but may identify as bisexual or asexual, transitioned later in life, rarely passed successfully as women, were considered to have been typical boys ("boyish") by their parents and teachers, and were very likely to report finding wearing women's clothes to be, or once had been, sexually arousing (85% of self-identified gynephilic MTF report erotic arousal to cross-dressing).

No other groupings had such strong statistical signals.

Attempts to find a third group fail, as every possible third group, based on MTF transsexual narratives, claims that they represent such a third group, show that they are in fact simply a subgroup of the second group, with nearly the same level of autogynephilia, the same age of transition, the same level (lack) of gender atypicality in childhood, etc.

When using statistics with people, one always expects "noise": false positives and false negatives: People misunderstand the questions, misinterpret their own feelings and behavior, prefer not to provide definite answers, wish to appear to better advantage, or simply like to introduce bogus answers to cause mischief. So the statistics can never be 0% vs. 100% in any study; but 15% vs. 85% is a very, very strong statistical signal and large effect size in psychology studies. In fact, this statistic says that even with the false response rate, "late transitioning" transwomen are over 550%, five and a half times (5.5X), more likely to report being sexually aroused by cross-dressing as those "early transitioners" who transition in their teens. Indeed, had these numbers been any closer to 0% vs. 100%, knowledgeable scientists / psychometricians / statisticians would have flagged the data in peer review of these papers as being "too good to be true", given well known real world difficulties in psychology research.

Science depends upon repeatability, and these results regarding sexual orientation and autogynephilia have been replicated by Buhrich (1977), Freund (1982), Blanchard (1985, 1987), Doorn (1994), Smith (2005), Lawrence (2005), and Nuttbrock (2009), in separate studies spanning four decades, collectively involving over a thousand transwomen to date. In fact, this is one of the most repeated and reconfirmed scientific finding regarding transsexuality. While Blanchard coined the term "autogynephilia" in the late '80s, the phenomena had been noted and studied before using various synonymous terms such as "fetishistic transvestism" and "fetishistic femmiphilia". This is not the only statistic that shows that there are two and only two types, of course, but is the single most important.

It is important to note that these statistical studies were following up on observational studies from the early to mid-20th Century that noted the same correlations, especially those of Magnus Hirschfeld (sexologist & LGBT rights activist and author of *Transvestites* in 1910), Dr. Christian Hamburger (the famous doctor who treated Christine Jorgensen, who took the feminine form of his name in his honor, in 1952), Dr. Harry Benjamin (a close friend of Hirschfeld and author of the famous 1966 book, *The Transsexual Phenomena*), Dr. Robert Stoller (who wrote *Sex and Gender* in 1968), Dr. Ethel Person (who collected her earlier research in her 1999 book *Sexual Century*), and Dr. Richard Green (who wrote *Sexual Identity Conflict in Children and Adults* in 1974). All of these clinicians and researchers clearly wrote about and described autogynephilic behavior and motivations in adult transitioning MTF transsexuals. All of them noted that very young transitioning MTF transsexuals did not exhibit an autogynephilic history, but were universally exclusively attracted to men.

For example, from his description of his "high intensity" category in his 1966 book, *The Transsexual Phenomena*, Benjamin wrote,

> *"Intensely desires relations with normal male as "female," if young. Later, libido low. May have been married and have children, by using fantasies in intercourse."*

Note that he describes "young" as exclusively androphilic, while "later", meaning older transitioners, being gynephilic, as evidenced by marriage to women and fathering children, accompanied by autogynephilic "fantasies in intercourse".

Science also depends upon multiple lines of reproducible evidence coming together to support a theory. In this case, we have that in abundance.

The second most important statistical evidence is biodemographics.

One of these is that transgender leanings tend to run in families, but not the same families. That is to say, that the two types are almost never found in the same family, but it is common for several transkid siblings to transition together, while it is common to find two autogynephilic males in the same family. Another biodemographic is that homosexual transsexuals, as a group, have more older brothers, and more brothers than sisters, than the general population and even gay men, while non-homosexual transsexuals have the same as the general population. This means that for both types, the condition has in-born factors, but not the same factors. There is no overlap between the two. This alone is powerful, and likely conclusive, evidence that the two taxons have differing etiologies.

The third statistical finding is that homosexual transsexuals are extremely unlikely to have paraphilic sexual interests, similar to non-transwomen, while autogynephilic transsexuals are very likely to have such paraphilic sexual interests such as Bondage&Discipline, 'forced feminization', latex clothing, auto-erotic asphyxiation, etc., at rates that exceed the base rate for non-transgendered men, and far exceed the base rate for women. Since paraphilias tend to cluster, that is, that if an individual has one paraphilia, they are more likely to have another, it suggests that autogynephilia may itself be a paraphilia.

Analogously, autogynephilic transsexuals and cross-dressers are very likely to also be gynandromorphophilic (preferentially or at least equally attracted to other transwomen as to women) while homosexual transsexuals are not.

An additional statistical finding is that the percentage of autogynephilic transsexuals in a country highly correlates with that country's Hofstede Index for Individualism vs. Collectivism. That is to say, that autogynephilic transsexuals are far less likely to transition in countries that place higher value on collective family responsibility, while homosexual transsexuals are still likely to transition. The countries with the highest Individualism score and thus the highest percentage of autogynephilic transsexuals are the English speaking nations. As Dr. Anne Lawrence, who discovered this relationship explains,

> *"As I suggested previously, the observed relationship between IDV and %NHS probably reflects the combined operation of at least two distinct factors. First, non-homosexual persons probably constitute larger apparent percentages of MtF transsexuals and gender dysphoric persons in more individualist societies because these societies place a higher value on individual self-expression (including cross-gender expression), despite the possible socially disruptive consequences of gender transition in men who are typically middle-aged, are often married, and have usually pursued traditionally masculine*

occupations. Second, homosexual persons probably constitute larger apparent percentages of MtF transsexuals and gender dysphoric persons in less individualistic (or collectivistic) societies because these societies place a higher value on inclusion and often provide socially approved transgender roles for pervasively feminine, androphilic gender dysphoric men."

There is a distinct bimodal distribution in the age of severe gender dysphoria (GD) onset into early and late and of age of obtaining surgery that correlates and demonstrates the separate life arcs of the two types.

Although not often discussed, there is data showing that homosexual transsexuals are genitally "avoidant", that is to say, that though they will joyfully have sexual relations with their boyfriends, as "bottoms", they assiduously avoid use, contact, and often even visual exposure, of their own pre-op genitalia. Autogynephilic transsexuals however usually have no such reservations, including active participation in penetrative vaginal and oral sex, often siring children, with their wives / girlfriends.

Just as men are far more likely to be autistic than women, autogynephiles are far more likely to be autistic than homosexual transsexuals. Further, on an autism scale, non-autistic men score slightly higher than women. Essentially the same scores are found for gynephilic vs. homosexual MTF transsexuals.

Group:	Men		Women	Gynephilic
Homosexual .				MTF N=129
MTF N=69				
Score (SD):	17.8 (6.8)	15.4 (5.7)	17.4 (7.4)	15.0 (5.6)

There is the curious statistic that while homosexual transsexuals have as a group, average IQ=100, while autogynephilic transsexuals exhibit, as a group, significantly higher IQ (121.7 in one clinical study). This is likely from a self-selection effect in which only those who can "afford" it, choose to transition. It is commonly noted that homosexual transsexuals are far more likely to be poor, homeless, and members of ethnic/racial minorities in Western nations, than autogynephilic transsexuals.

Clinical comparisons support the oft noted observation that homosexual transsexuals 'pass' better than autogynephilic transsexuals, that they are physically more feminine than autogynephilic transsexuals (d=0.7) .

There is growing evidence that homosexual transsexuals (both MTF and FtM) have cross-sex brain features that can be measured using modern MRI scans while non-homosexual transsexuals do not, but may have other features, not found in controls that are not sexually dimorphic. This result, first obtained in 2011, confirmed predictions made by Blanchard in 2008. Since then, multiple papers on the subject have been published. In 2016, in a review of the papers then available, Guillamon et al offered this chief conclusion at the end of the paper,

"The review of the available data seems to support two existing hypotheses: (1) a brain-restricted intersexuality in homosexual MtFs and FtMs and (2) Blanchard's insight on the existence of two brain phenotypes that differentiate "homosexual" and "nonhomosexual" MtFs"

The review of all of the available brain structure research fully supports the Two Type Taxonomy. In light of this, the authors recommend that future researchers take care to distinguish between the two types, lamenting that some studies in the review had not made this distinction, and further, that it is important that the control groups also be concordant with sexual orientation,

"The study of mixed samples implicitly assumes that transsexuals are a homogeneous group. This is far from the truth with respect to the onset of GD and sexual orientation. … These observations signify that control groups in studies of the transsexual brain must be homogeneous in regards to sexual orientation."

Although very tentative, there is 2D:4D (measurement of the fingers of the hand – comparing pointing finger to ring finger length) evidence that MTF homosexual transsexuals have feminized hands indicating that they had lower testosterone exposure in utero than control men while late onset MTF transsexuals do not. Even more intriguing is the data that suggests that late onset (androphilic) FtM are not only very different from early onset, but are actually MORE feminine than control women.

Finally, MTF homosexual transsexuals, have a distinctive hormonal (Lutinizing Hormone) response to acute introduction and withdrawal of estrogen which is similar to natal females, while non-homosexual transsexuals respond the same as heterosexual non-transgendered men. This is laboratory diagnostic "proof" of the two type taxonomy.

7 HOMOSEXUAL TRANSSEXUALS

Let us explore the "typical" homosexual transsexual.

The typical (one might say, 'stereotypical') Male-To-Female (MTF) homosexual transsexual was called a "sissy" by her peers growing up. She avoided rough & tumble activities. Her primary social circle consisted of one or two girls. She actively participated in girl's games and imaginary play. Her parents were embarrassed by her femininity, and may or may not have sought professional help in trying to discourage her behavior. As a young teen, she became interested in girls fashion and make-up, often exploring how she might look as a girl by dressing up and experimenting with make-up, with occasional trips out shopping or hanging out with her friends. This did not, of course, involve erotic cross-dressing. She had crushes on BOYS(!) at school. Her peers thought she might be homosexual. She was hassled, perhaps even bullied, by homophobic boys, but otherwise was reasonably popular in her chosen circle. She sought out opportunities to interact with small children and infants, taking on babysitting jobs. As she approached adulthood, looking at her own nature, her potential future, both romantic and economic, made a rational decision to transition to living as a girl so as to grow up to be a woman socially. Her family may or may not have disowned her in late adolescence. As she is naturally feminine and passes quite well, she found that she was socially and romantically more successful as a woman. She actively dated heterosexual men while pre-op, but assiduously avoided direct contact with her penis, finding that emotionally uncomfortable. Being young and lacking capital, she lived several years as a woman, taking feminizing hormones, before having SRS to improve her sex life, replacing genitalia that she didn't use with those that she did. She may or may not have found a husband and adopted children. From Dr. Robert Stoller's 1968 book, *Sex and Gender*, starting on page 190,

> *"Let us briefly describe a typical male transsexual. The patient is twenty-five years old. She is dyed-blonde, well-rounded "woman" who in none of the ordinary mannerisms of life (smoking cigarettes, walking, crossing her legs, blowing her nose, gesticulating, etc.) in any way reveals she was ever a male. She points out that she had the same mannerisms when living as a male, when she seemed bizarre. She recalls no time in life of not wanting to be a girl, of not feeling extremely feminine, of not having interests and daydreams that seemed to her the same as those of normal girls. Her earliest memories, starting around the age of three, already show this very feminine attitude. As a boy, she was treated with ridicule by the other boys, despite which she maintained her same feminine behavior. … her daydreams from the start were that she was a woman being made love to by a man. … She hated to masturbate and says she did so only once a year or less, not because of conscious guilt but because it so concretely demonstrated her anatomical maleness. … She began going out with men and having sexual relations. However, she never permitted a man to touch or see her genitalia, since they were such a source of shame; she defined as normal any man who made no such attempts. … Some months before I first met her, she made contact with an operated transsexual, who suggested that they live together (not sexually, of course). She did so, and at the point for the first time she went through the preparations that were to lead to her being able to pass successfully as a female. … She was so successful that she very shortly found herself a job, being hired unsuspectingly as a woman. … The patient has now married and hopes to adopt children."*

The key diagnostic features are sustained femininity beginning in early childhood that persists into adolescence and exclusive androphilia (sexual and romantic attraction to men) and an absence of autogynephilia. The median age of transition for MTF of this type is 20 years old, with a typical range of early puberty to mid-20's, though recently some are transitioning before puberty if they have supportive parents. Nearly all transition full-time before the age of 25 and it is unheard of to find one who transitions full time after age 30. Thinking about these individuals as so like girls/women that they might as well be that sex offers a straight forward and insightful way of viewing them.

Similar to the above, a homosexual Female-to-Male (FtM) transsexual was called a "tomboy" growing up. Most of his friends were boys and other 'tomboyish' girls, playing boy games, into stories and images of masculine heroes (or villains), loved loud, boisterous rough and tumble games. He typically hated playing girl games, especially "house" or other make-believe games. He hated to dress up in feminine clothes. As a teen, he was interested in sports, athletics, skate-boards, fast cars or motorcycles, and pretty GIRLS! As a young adult, he may have identified as a "butch" lesbian, but hated his body, especially his chest. He easily slid over to living as a man and began taking HRT and had top surgery. He may or may not have had bottom surgery. He dated both straight and bisexual identified women. He may or may not have married a straight or bisexual woman and became a step-father to her children from a prior marriage.

The key diagnostic features are sustained masculinity beginning in early childhood that persisted into adolescence and exclusive gynephilia (sexual and romantic attraction to women). The median age of transition is 25 to 30 with a range of early puberty (and even younger in recent times) to late-30s.

8 AUTOGYNEPHILIC TRANSSEXUALS AND TRANSVESTITES

The prototypical autogynephilic ("Non-Homosexual" or "Late Onset") transsexual was accepted as a boy as a child. She was often a "loner", finding her hobbies and reading to be more rewarding, but still willing and ready to participate in rough & tumble play. She often envied girls and observed them more often than most boys. As she entered puberty, she began erotic cross-dressing in private, often masturbating while crossed-dressed, usually with just lingerie. She found this shameful and hid her cross-dressing as best she could. She entertained thoughts of living as a woman, often in very sexually idealized, socially stereotyped, situations. As a young adult, she dated women, often finding it necessary to imagine that she was female to "perform". She typically hid this fact from her dates. In an effort to deny her autogynephilic desire for femininity, she may have chosen to pursue a stereotypically masculine, or even hyper-masculine, career such as the military or police. She fell in love and found that the previously growing desire to live as a woman abated for a while. She married and had children. Her need to cross-dress and use autogynephilic ideation later returned, as the first blush of their romance matured into committed love. She agonized about it obsessively, trying alternatively to push it out of her thoughts and trying to appease it by cross-dressing. In public, she chose to dress and groom herself in stereotypically and unmistakably masculine fashion, with perhaps even a mustache or full beard. At one point, perhaps in her early 30s, or in her late 50s, a set-back or other significant personal change brought all of these feelings to the fore... and she made the fateful decision that she could no longer ignore her sexuality. After having tried to ignore the cognitive dissonance between her successful social identity as a man, husband, and father, and her obligatory autogynephilic image of being female, she concluded that the female image is her "true" self. She then made steps to begin counseling with a gender therapist, obtained prescription for feminizing hormones, began electrolysis and other procedures to effect a more feminine appearance, and then began the painful steps to living full-time socially as a "transsexual", since she didn't pass very well and had too many social connections who know of her previous status as a man to be truly stealth. She had SRS within a short time of nominally living as a woman, as she was impatient, feeling like she had waited long enough in her previous life as a man. Her wife most likely demanded a divorce.

Although they may appear to be a different taxon to an inexperienced clinician, there is a subset of autogynephilic transgendered population for whom their autogynephilia overshadows their underlying gynephilia, typically presenting younger and as "asexual", that is to say, that they show no or only limited romantic interest in other people. Many have schizotypal personalities.

Before transition, the natural behavior of autogynephilic MTF transsexuals is gender typical, easily passing as typical straight men, often marrying women, fathering children, and successful in stereotypically masculine and even hyper-masculine (e.g. Navy Seal) careers. It is not uncommon for them to exhibit homophobic and sexist attitudes. As it takes years for the cross-gender identity to form and establish itself, the modal age for transition is 35 to 40 years old, the mean is between 40 to 45, with a range of early 20's to very old age. After transition, they may identify as lesbian, asexual, bisexual, or even straight women, including marrying men. Thinking about autogynephilic MTF transsexuals as "male bodied people who love women and (romantically) want to become what they love" offers a more accurate and more richly informative way to understand them.

The key diagnostic feature here is that of autogynephilia, sexual arousal and romantic attachment to the thought of being female/feminine. Autogynephilia is an Erotic Target Location Error in which one's usual uncomplicated sexual orientation, gynephilia (attraction to women), is mapped onto oneself instead of sought after in others. The word comes from "auto", meaning 'self', "gyne", meaning 'female', and "philia" meaning 'love'. In other words, the "love of oneself as a woman". In the simplest analysis, autogynephilia is a set of sexual interests and behaviors that includes the more commonly understood term, transvestism / cross-dresser on one end of the 'transgender spectrum' and AGP transsexual on the other.

Although transvestism is the most common expression, it can exist without it. For example, a fairly common autogynephilic sexual fantasy is for a man to imagine oneself as a nude woman. One might also include an admirer in the room, but the focus is on the physical self. One can't use female garments to aid in a fantasy where one is nude! Blanchard's study of such autogynephiles has shown that the more sexually aroused by, focused, a man is on having a vagina, the more likely he is to go onto to transition and request Sex Reassignment Surgery (SRS). After all, if an autogynephile is satisfied by temporarily assuming the clothed form of a woman, the more likely he is to be comfortable with remaining simply a transvestite. But, if one's sexuality depends on obligatory autogynephilic ideation of being anatomically female, then one grows ever hungrier to realize that fantasy in real life. Of course, both forms of autogynephilic expression often coexist. After all, one could fantasize about being female bodied, underneath that glamorous Versace dress. In sexual relations with their girlfriends and wives, a common fantasy for an autogynephilic man is to imagine that he is a lesbian having sex with his lesbian partner.

I had a friend in Jr. High. Let's call him MJ. MJ was the ugliest boy in the class. No joke, no insult intended, he was. He was also short, clumsy and klutzy. There was nothing feminine about him, though he was quiet and withdrawn. He had a funny way of slurring his words that suggested a birth defect like a split palate. Because of this nearly no one liked him as he seemed to have an invisible sign stuck to his back that read, "kick me". He tended to drive away potential friends with his tendency to whining and neediness. He could count on one hand people who would be civil to him. I was one of them.

Our freshman year in high school, a group of mischievous "popular" (i.e. "mean") girls set out to play match-maker for one of the girls in school, let's call her JM. JM was the ugliest girl in the class. No joke, no insult intended, she was. JM was loud, boisterous, exuberant, and you couldn't help but like her. The match-makers settled on my friend MJ as her match, thinking it a funny (and cruel) joke. But the joke was on them. They had indeed made a perfect match. Her outgoing personality brought his personality out. His quiet thoughtfulness calmed and soothed her over-exuberance. They were literally joined at the hip, often walking side by side with a hand in each other's back pocket. Together, they canceled out the ugly and were the cutest couple on campus - as in the way that really ugly, funny looking but lovable dogs are "cute". One couldn't help but smile seeing them together, so happy and in love. They married right after graduation… but I had moved prior to that, so lost touch.

Years spin by…. and I end up back in touch with them, still together. But now, MJ is fawning all over me, saying how "lucky" I was to have transitioned so early, as a teen in high school… yes… he, at the age of 40, had decided it was high time to transition.

I counseled caution, knowing that he was never going to pass. I asked, "How are you so sure that you are a woman?"

"Because every time we have sex, I have to imagine myself as a lesbian to have any response."

I was floored! MJ's "proof" that he was a 'woman inside' was simple autogynephilic ideation. It had worn at him over the years. He first tried to use antipsychotics, tranquilizers, alcohol, anything to push back the shame that he felt for his sexuality. But with each passing year, the need to do more to include that aspect of his inner life as part of his everyday life grew. First, he wore skirts privately at home. Then in public. Never popular, he drove away all of his remaining friends due to his constant obsessing over whether this meant that he was a woman or a man. Then, at the age of 40, he was asking me for advice about hormones. I told him to see a doc… and looked over his head at poor JM, who though still loving MJ, knew this was the end of their marriage, their high school sweethearts, 26 year romance.

MJ's experience is similar to most autogynephilic transsexuals, in that autogynephilia is both a spectrum and a progression from secret transvestite to open transsexual. As an old joke in the transgender community has it:

What's the difference between a transvestite and a transsexual?

Two years!

There are five major categories of autogynephilic expression / interests: Transvestic, Anatomic, Behavioral, Interpersonal, and Physiological.

Transvestic, crossdressing to simulate the appearance of a woman, is the most common, or at least visible, type. It is listed in the DSM as "transvestic fetishism" but this is a misnomer, since it is not a fetish per se. A fetish is the use of objects as an erotic focus (e.g. shoes), as a substitute for a live person. But here, a live person is most definitely still the focus, themselves. Transvestic autogynephilia is an erotic focus on temporarily changing one's appearance to that of a woman. The clothes are not a true fetish object, just a means to the appearance change. A more extreme form of this is to wear latex/silicone femmeform 'skin' and 'mask' that cover much of or the entire body. While commonly found in autogynephilic transsexuals, not all males who experience transvestic autogynephilia become transsexual, most remain cross-dressers.

Anatomic autogynephilia is sexual arousal and desire to physically embody a female, with breasts and/or genitalia. It has been hypothesized to be the root cause of autogynephilic transsexuality. Research suggests that those who experience complete anatomic autogynephilia are the most likely to want, and later to actually, socially transition. Though other research suggests that interpersonal autogynephilia may also play a large part in such decisions. Conversely, there are also those who, for lack of a better term, experience "partial" autogynephilia, in that they want to have women's breasts, but retain male genitalia. Typically, those who experience partial autogynephilia, choose not to socially transition full-time, but may live as 'gender fluid' or 'non-binary' and take low doses of feminizing hormones.

Behavioral autogynephilia is arousal to activities culturally associated with women. It can be almost anything, from getting one's hair or nails done at the beauty parlor in the company of women, shopping for women's clothing while cross-dressed, to speaking or singing in a feminine voice.

Interpersonal autogynephilia is arousal to the thought of being accepted as a woman, admired as a woman, to receiving admiring gazes from others, to having sex with others as a woman, even to having sex with men, even though they aren't actually physically attracted to men. This last is also called autogynephilic pseudo-androphilia or pseudo-bisexuality, and is fairly common. In these cases, the individual must be dressed as a woman, or be post-operative, to experience themselves as being a woman during the sexual encounter in order to be aroused in the company of men; the focus remains on the female self, the man is only there to admire that female self.

Physiological autogynephilia is arousal to the thought or simulation of female physiological functions. It can include sitting down to urinate, pretending to have menstrual symptoms (taking Midol for imagined cramps, bloating, bleeding, using pads, and even placing tampons into one's anus), pretending to be pregnant (pillows under maternity clothing, etc.), nursing a baby, and so on.

Autogynephilia often co-exists with other unusual erotic interests, most notably masochism including autoerotic-asphyxiation, sexual submission, bondage, and humiliation. Many combine the two where it becomes an intense interest in "forced feminization" fantasies and enactments in which an attractive woman "forces" them to dress and take on female "submissive" roles such as "french maid", etc. Research shows that about one of four autogynephiles have such interests.

Any individual autogynephilic male may experience any of the above in any combination and intensity. These sexual arousal patterns and interests usually surface in puberty, though occasionally they may surface earlier. Their overt sexual nature is most observable in adolescence, when these behaviors and fantasies are often enacted along with masturbation. As an autogynephilic individual matures, the overt sexual nature may become less apparent, while the need for the behavior, especially crossdressing and MTF transition, grows. Thus, erotic transvestism and autogynephilic transsexuality are both a continuum and a progression. Autogynephilia, like most aspects of sexuality, can NOT be "cured". There is no known treatment to stop one from being autogynephilic.

It is important to note that autogynephilic males are not naturally feminine, in either appearance or behavior. Rather, they find simulating the appearance and behavior of women to be sexually and affectionally rewarding. Thus, over time, dedicated transvestites and autogynephilic transsexuals work to perfect their appearance and presentation as women, or rather more often, their ideal woman, but it doesn't come naturally.

Autogynephilic transsexuals will often spend every last dollar they can lay hand to in their quest for their perfect female self. It is very much as if they are both spending and gifting on both themselves and to the 'other woman'. As well as spending rather lavishly on women's clothing, they will spend tens of thousands of dollars on each of multiple procedures including; Facial Feminization Surgery (FFS), breast implants, hair removal (beard and even scrotum), hair transplants (to cover male pattern baldness), tracheal shave (to remove Adam's Apple), voice feminization surgery, Sex Reassignment Surgery (SRS), etc. Insurance may or may not pay for SRS, but is very unlikely to pay for much else. The least expensive item will be feminizing Hormone Replacement Therapy. And speaking of 'therapy', they will spend thousands on weekly visits to a gender therapist. They may also spend thousands on voice coaching, comportment coaching, etc., in order to improve their feminine presentation, since, as I mentioned above, it doesn't come naturally.

Since, as children, teens, and young adults, autogynephilic individuals do not exhibit naturally feminine behavior, and may in fact be quite naturally masculine, even hypermasculine (e.g. Navy Seal / fireman / police officer) right up to the moment that they announce that they are transgendered, this is why parents, siblings, and wives of autogynephilic transsexuals are so often surprised when an autogynephilic transsexual announces their intention to transition. Over time, their secret autogynephilic ideal of being female has warred with their original identity of being a man, until finally, the cognitive dissonance between the two must be resolved by abandoning their previous gender identity as a man. They may then state that they had always been feminine but hid it. But no one who is truly feminine can "hide" that fact from close associates for years on end. What they mean is that they always felt a **desire** to be feminine/female and hid that desire.

An important aspect of any sexual orientation is that of love, romance, emotional bonding. In a very real sense, autogynephilic cross-dressers and transwomen fall in love with their feminine self-image and want to give her more life and expression, not unlike the way that a straight man who loves his wife wishes to provide her a safe and comforting home. Autogynephiles often have trouble expressing their feelings, finding it mysterious and confusing. This is why they cling to the notion that they "feel like a woman", as short-hand for their love for their idealized feminine self-image.

However, this behavior of erotic and romantic attachment to their feminine self-image is not "narcissism" in the personality sense. Narcissism as a personality trait is an exaggerated view of one's own importance/worthiness to and/or in relation/comparison to others. While it may occur in some autogynephiles, just as it occurs in non-autogynephiles, there is no causal link or correlation.

Autogynephilia is an Erotic Target Location Error, in which the erotic object, femaleness / femininity, is sought after on one's self, in addition to, or even as a substitute for, other people. It simultaneously depends upon and competes with heterosexual interest in women. Because of this, autogynephilia is not found in exclusively homosexual males (nor in heterosexual females, for the same reason). This is important in that there are two etiologies leading to MTF transsexuality, one is autogynephilia, as discussed here, the other is found in extremely feminine, exclusively "homosexual" males, who from early childhood, clearly act like and wish to be female. Once again, think: Caitlin Jenner vs. Laverne Cox. This other homosexual type is NOT autogynephilic. Their need to transition is based on their natural femininity and need to fit into society better. These two types of MTF transsexuals should not be confused with each other, but often are by the media, the public, and even many in the 'transgender community'.

As well as being attracted to women, most autogynephiles are also attracted to transwomen, especially to those who are more physically and behaviorally feminine (i.e. to the "homosexual transsexual" type) who are still 'pre-op' called "gynandromorphs" in the scientific literature. This attraction, called gynandromorphophilia (GAMP), often exceeds their attraction to women, and finds expression in interest in "she-male" pornography. This is both a direct attraction and a wishful projection, a desire both to make love to and to embody, to be like these young, beautiful transwomen.

An interesting thing about autogynephilia is that it tends to run in families. It's quite common to find two brothers, or father and son, who only after years of hiding their shameful secret, find out about each other. This suggests that there may be something genetic, or epigenetic, which leads to autogynephilia.

9 AUTOANDROPHILIC FEMALE-TO-MALE TRANSSEXUALS AND TRANSVESTITES

The rarest type of transsexual is the bisexual or gay male identified FtM type, though it may be becoming more common as the stigma attached to being transsexual decreases. Before transition, the natural behavior of non-homosexual / autoandrophilic FtM may be quite variable, but is usually less "butch" than exclusively gynephilic FtM transsexuals. Their families would likely describe them as having been very typical girls, with some tomboyish interests, comfortable being feminine (dresses, make-up, nail polish, etc.). Their sexuality is most likely to be also variable over time, where they may find men or women more attractive as partners at different times in their lives. Overt erotic cross-dressing occurs only rarely, but other aspects of autoandrophilia may be found in their fantasy life (e.g. erotic interest in Yaoi Manga) or having idealized crushes on FtM transmen (the mirror of autogynephiles' attraction to transwomen).

The key diagnostic features are conventional femininity to mild transient tomboyishness in early childhood and androphilia. Although autoandrophilic, finding direct evidence to it is difficult without deeply exploring their sexual fantasy life.

Dr. Robert Stoller wrote an interesting paper, that sheds light on androphilic transgender experience. But best to let one of the cases speak for him/herself:

"Today my sex life is mostly satisfied by masturbation, with transvestite episodes occasionally providing a pleasant stimulus to masturbation. I've dressed as a man, replete with moustache, and had my partner call me by a man's name. I take pleasure in being called by a man's name. Dressed as a

man, I've sucked my partner's penis. I felt myself, during the experience, to be a gay male."

"One perversity, perhaps, is that I like the idea of looking like a rather feminine male."

The theory that non-homosexual FtM transsexuals and transvestites are autoandrophilic is not without its critics. Blanchard in particular has instead suggested that they just have autohomoerotic fantasies of themselves as gay men. But is that really a different phenomenon or just a different name for it?

Recent research has shown that autogynephilic males can experience essentially the same thing as "Interpersonal Autogynephilia", in fact, many of them do, having fantasies in which they are lesbian. And no, one can't say that they aren't the same thing. Frankly, if males can experience autogynephilia as the result of an erotic target location error, by simple symmetry, we would expect that females can also experience autoandrophilia as a result of an erotic target location error.

Need proof that women can experience erotic target location errors? Consider amputee "devotees" and "wannabees", people who are both sexually attracted to amputees and want to become an amputee. While most are men, there are women. Are we to say that female wannabees experience a different phenomenon just because they are female? Seriously? I prefer to use Occam's razor and avoid unnecessary sexist ideology

10 EROTIC TARGET LOCATION ERRORS

Autogynephilia and autoandrophilia has been theorized to be caused by an Erotic Target Location Error in which the erotic target, usually other people, is locating within the self by error. If this theory is true, it predicts that men who are both gynephilically attracted to female amputees and have a deep desire to have a limb, such an arm or leg, removed (xenomelia) to be like their erotic target, would also be likely to want to be female and have other autogynephilic arousal patterns. In one of the few studies to test this prediction, we see exactly that, as described by Lawrence,

"Recently, First (2005) used semistructured telephone interviews to survey 52 persons who had expressed a wish to become an amputee or who had succeeded in doing so. About two thirds of participants were recruited from Internet discussion groups and about one third from referrals by other participants. Forty-seven (90%) participants were male, 4 (8%) were female, and 1 was intersexed and raised as a male; 32 (62%) participants reported that they were heterosexual and the remainder reported that they were homosexual or bisexual. First (2005) noted that the high proportion of nonheterosexual participants was "partly explained by the fact that nine of the subjects were referred to the study by one subject who was himself homosexual, eight of whom were also homosexual" (p. 921). Nine (17%) participants had undergone a major limb amputation. Forty-eight (92%) participants had pretended to be an amputee and 45 (87%) acknowledged sexual attraction to amputees. Fifteen (29%) participants reported other paraphilic interests, including 8 (15%) with transvestic fetishism. Ten (19%) participants reported they had sometimes wished to be the opposite sex or felt that they were in the body of the wrong sex; of these, 7 (13%) participants had crossed-dressed, not including the 8 participants who had cross-dressed in connection with transvestic fetishism. Six (12%) participants had considered

sex reassignment and 1 (2%) had undergone sex reassignment."

How likely are we to find in any random group of only 52 people, a post-op transsexual and six more that have thought about it? How about finding 15% who report erotic arousal to cross-dressing? And add to 13% more that cross-dress and experience some gender dysphoria? Looking at the above description, at least 15 of the 52 showed some level of gender dysphoria. Though we can't tell from the paragraph, I'd predict that all 15 (possibly 18) were heterosexual, which if true, would mean that 15 out of 32 people (47%) reported gender dysphoria or autogynephilic arousal. But, at the very least, 15 out of 52 "wannabe" people (29%) reported such.

So, Erotic Target Location Error theory's prediction that "wannabes" will also more likely to be autogynephilic and gender dysphoric than would be expected by random chance, is very strongly supported. Thus, the theory of Erotic Target Location Errors explaining autogynephilia is also supported by the data.

Some researchers have suggested that "wannabes" are suffering from a disorder akin to somatoparaphrenia, where people deny ownership of a paralyzed limb. Somatoparaphrenia can be treated using a technique in which caloric vestibular stimulation (CVS), involving pouring cold water into the ear canal induces sensations in the brain. The flow of water induces an illusion of motion, and is thought to stimulate regions of the brain that create a mental map of the body. The hypothesis is that the parts of the brain that form the somatosensory map of the limb that the individual wishes to have removed is somehow disordered in a similar manner as somatoparaphrenia. If CVS works to relieve the desire for limb amputation, this would contradict the very strong evidence that "wannabeism" is an erotic target location error. A recent paper showed that CVS does NOT reduce the desire, supporting the paraphilic hypothesis and not supporting the somatoparaphrenic hypothesis.

11 ORIGINS OF GENDER IDENTITY

The widely held conception that transsexuals suffer from an innate, biological, disturbance of gender identity is at best only a secondary effect. The cause must necessarily be different for autogynephilic and young transitioning (feminine homosexual transsexuals) transkids, as their etiologies are unrelated. Clearly, almost all people do identify as members of one or the other social gender, nearly always congruently with their biological sex. But does that necessarily mean that self-identification with a given social gender is directly the result of biological brain sex as many transsexuals claim?

Human beings are not computers, with an unchangeable Read Only Memory that includes an ID serial number and name. Instead, we must learn, or create, our identities as individuals. Likewise there is no innate neural circuit that may be unambiguously read out that indicates one's gender. Instead, we must infer this from the outside. But many MTF transsexuals, most of whom, in the Western nations, are clearly male and masculine in both behavior and appearance before (and most often after) transition declare that they do have a sense of having an innate "female gender identity" despite all appearances to the contrary. This seeming contradiction with the experience of the rest of human society begs explanation.

Children naturally gender segregate, play in same-sex groups, beginning around age three. By age five, this preference is pronounced. This segregation appears to be based on play style compatibility. These play styles are not simply based on toy preference or sex role stereotyping, but on differences of social skills and interaction. Girls are self-segregating on their "pro-social" interactions, specifically, the use of polite suggestions and acceptance of others' such polite suggestions, a give and take that seeks to maximize social harmony, while boys make direct demands and are disruptive. Feminine boys are noted to prefer female playmates around the same age. These boys may also be searching out playmates with compatible play styles, as "boys play too rough" as Dr. Green documented. The girls may in turn be accepting of these feminine boys on this very same basis, as these boys' evident pro-social skills and play preferences mirror their own.

As children are largely sexually undifferentiated until adolescence, save for genitalia, which remain largely hidden beneath clothing, they must use other clues for gender attribution of their peers. Sex specific clothing serves as one such gendered clue. So does play style and play content preference. For young feminine boys, this latter gendered clue provides strong evidence, to themselves, that they may be better off as girls, may in fact be girls, despite others insistence on their being boys. Feminine boys are notable for their preference for female roles in play acting, being "the mommy" or the "nurse" over being the "daddy". As these feminine boys may then wish to be considered to be girls by others, so as to enjoy greater social acceptance within their preferred female circle, they may also prefer girls' clothing to provide further gender clues that are compatible with their growing awareness of their greater similarity to their female playmates.

Sounds like these boys are headed toward growing up to be a transsexual?

Nope!

Most such feminine boys do not grow up to be transsexual. They grow up to be feminine gay men. Between the ages of seven and twelve, future gay boys show less femininity as they accommodate to the modern gay male identity.

However, this early experience identifying with her female playmates often is the earliest awareness of a "female gender identity" and of cross-dressing in the very rare child that is to grow up to be a homosexual transsexual; As she grows older, far from becoming less feminine, she becomes more so.

Thus, the source of gender identification and later of social gender identity for homosexual transsexuals is found in the process of comparison of their own personalities and social interactions with the majority of men and women. A transkid observes that she is much more like her female friends, in nearly every respect, and unlike her male associates. She comes to feel that she would be better off as a woman, and after finding greater social ease and acceptance post transition, finds confirmation that indeed she is more comfortable as a woman and enjoys an easy détente with society that accepts her womanly presentation.

In contrast, autogynephilic males do not commonly exhibit feminine behavior and identification as young children. They experience a typically masculine boyhood, choosing and being accepted by other masculine boys as playmates. However, as adults, in transition, they report that they are "women inside". They insist that all external appearances notwithstanding, they have a "hidden female gender identity" that is at odds with their external anatomy and behavior. Where does this seeming contradiction come from?

The most parsimonious hypothesis would be that they are lying. Autogynephilia drives these men to want to feminize their bodies, but the medical system denies access to such procedures unless they lie, confabulate histories that more closely approximate feminine androphilic transsexual histories. Indeed, we know that this was historically true in some, but not all clinics. But since it is no longer true, that autogynephiles are actively accepted and accommodated in today's boutique medical care system, the simple prevarication hypothesis cannot provide the full answer.

Most autogynephilic transsexuals are sincere and honest in their assertion that they do experience a definite internal sense of having a "female gender identity". Assuming that they are not lying, could there be another explanation?

The author has the unusual luck in having known, of having been on friendly terms with, a classmate during Jr. High and High School that transitioned at age 40, as I discussed previously. Most revealingly, when pressed for reasons, MJ said that she knew that he was a "woman inside" because ever since meeting her future wife, she had used, needed, the fantasy that she was a lesbian, a female having sex with another female, while having otherwise conventional heterosexual intercourse. MJ literally equated obligatory autogynephilic ideation with having a "female gender identity"!!!

Conversations with other late transitioning transsexuals reveals similar admissions. If every time an autogynephilic transsexual sees herself, in her mind's eye, in a sexual situation as obligatorily female, this would provide strong evidence that she is indeed "female inside". No amount of masculine behavior, manners, or appearance could countermand such an immediate and complete "proof" of her "identity", once that connection is accepted.

The equation of autogynephilic ideation with "female gender identity" also answers another question regarding autogynephilic transsexual life arcs, the issue of late transitioning. After all, if these individuals had in fact a female gender identity, why then would they wait so long to transition, often after years of marriage and career? The answer is that they did not in fact have such a female gender identity, or even identify with women, at first. This lack of identification with women often is evidenced by sexism and male chauvinism.

Well known and respected gender therapist, Dr. Anne Vitale, noted this internalized bias and tightly held sense of entitlement in one of her essays on the phenomena,

> *"One of the most interesting aspects I have found in my work with genetic males struggling with deep-seated gender dysphoria is ingrained sexism. Although it would seem to be completely out-of-place in this population, the fact that it is present and present almost exclusively in genetic males tells us a great deal about how some men feel about femininity and about aspects of the nature of gender dysphoria. As a general rule, the men I am speaking about present for therapy appearing decidedly male, often to the point of wearing full beards. In addition, they are more often than [homosexual transsexuals] to present [as] married, to have children, and to have never considered having a homosexual experience. … There are those that think that what women do — those social behaviors that differentiate them from men — are frivolous and unimportant. Indeed, there are those who take this belief to the point where they feel that women are less than men and are embarrassed over wanting to be like them. Interestingly, these people have no trouble at all with wearing very feminine apparel — as long as they can do it in complete privacy or with the above mentioned male bravado. … Perhaps the most insidious form of sexism resides in the gender dysphoric male who has attained a highly respected position in a male dominated profession. These people routinely tell me that although women are now allowed a certain professional tolerance, the real players are still men."*

They, like the homosexual transsexual, had compared their own personalities and social interactions during childhood and adolescence, with the majority of men and women, and originally found that they best fit in as men, that they were in fact, men. Indeed, this process is likely to be universal in early childhood as to go unnoticed in non-transsexual people. But for the autogynephilic individual in adolescence, a cognitive dissonance is created by the growing awareness of autogynephilic arousal. This may be accommodated by partial or complete cross-dressing in private, perhaps for life. But for those few who experience complete and obligatory autogynephilic ideation as their only means for sexual arousal, the cognitive dissonance between their socially formed identity as men and their internal sexual self-image as female preys on them. This creates a struggle that may be evidenced by a "flight into hypermasculinity" as he tries to fight back the need to be female in erotic situations. As sexuality is notoriously refractory, it is the socially formed identity that must buckle if the internal struggle is to be relieved. The result is an acceptance of, and then staunchly defended, sense of a "female gender identity".

This is not a "gender identity" in the usual sense. It is instead, an autoerotic body image. But, as the idealized autoerotic body image competes with, is directly contradictory to, the socially formed identity, the inner sense of the difference between the two is blurred for the autogynephilic transsexual. It becomes conceptually easier, far less painful, to accept that she is a woman inside, has always been a woman inside, than to remain consciously aware of the cognitive dissonance between being socially and sexually a masculine man and obligatorily, through no choice of her own, always a woman in her inner sexual life.

About five years ago, I got an email from a transwoman, an 'older transitioner' who acknowledged without reservation that there was a "correlation" between later transition / gynephilia (non-exclusive androphilic) transwomen and autogynephilia, while tacitly acknowledging that exclusively androphilic early transitioners do not. This was great, but not too surprising, since four out of five such transwomen acknowledge experiencing autogynephilia either currently, or in the past. But she asked, does it mean causation? That is to say, is autogynephilia the prime mover in causing gynephilic (and bisexual / asexual) transwomen to become gender dysphoric and develop a 'female identity'?

I would have thought it was obvious that it does, and that we don't need to explain why. But, no, sillyolme, nothing in science is self-evident. One really does need to explore the question fairly, making the assumption, the null hypothesis that it does not, then look to see if the evidence supports that null hypothesis. Only if the data fails to support the null hypothesis should we state that it does.

Let's start at the beginning shall we? First, does autogynephilia exist? Yes, we need to ask this first, as it can't be a cause of gender dysphoria if it doesn't exist. And, indeed, many 'older transitioners' insist that autogynephilia does not exist. Well, that one is easily answered, because we have at least 100 years of sexologist observations of a minority of males who definitely become sexually aroused when wearing women's clothing and/or when thinking of themselves being or becoming female. Consider this typical bit of autogynephilic erotica of a teenaged male experiencing an autogynephilic episode from Richard Ekins book Male Femaling – A grounded theory approach to cross-dressing and sex-changing,

"... I was 13 when I stepped, quivering with excitement into a pair of French knickers belonging to my sister. I ejaculated almost immediately...

The feeling was glorious and yet quite alarming and I felt as though I was leaking urine. ... Some three days after this first 'event' I got home from school to find my mother out. I went upstairs to do my homework and through the half-opened door of my mother's bedroom I saw, hanging over a chair, a pair of her pink directoire knickers, obviously discarded in a hurry as she changed before going out. That soft gleaming bundle turned my whole body and senses into a jelly-like state of desire and longing. I had to wear them, to try and see if I was all right. Would it happen again? My answer was there almost immediately in my swift gathering erection as I struggled out of my clothes. ..."

We can find hundreds, thousands, of such examples, very often showing that this behavior is most noted in early adolescence, but continues into adulthood. In fact, we have an entire genre of erotic fiction and images (still and motion picture porn) dedicated to the tastes of autogynephilic adult male individuals. These examples and the males that experience it are common enough that they also form organizations to join together to support each other emotionally and even politically. So, no, we can't say that autogynephilia does not exist. The null hypothesis is easily proven wrong. Autogynephilia in some males exists.

OK, now that we know that autogynephilia exists in some males, we can take a known group of autogynphilic males, conduct in-depth interviews into just what sorts of things they erotically respond to that the majority, non-autogynephilic, males don't. From that we can construct trial psychometric inventories, test items (questions), for an autogynephilia scale, so that we can measure the degree of and autogynephilic factors (types) present in, autogynephilic males. Then carefully test and validate it against known autogynephilic males and a set of control males.

However, some transwomen insist that autogynephilia can't be the cause of their transsexual identity, because autogynephilia is common, perhaps near universal, in females. Thus, that would demonstrate that autogynephilia is just part of normal female sexuality.

Does autogynephilia exist in females? Now, remember, we START with the null hypothesis. So, assuming it does NOT exist, can we find (credible) evidence that would disprove the null hypothesis? First, how many sexologists have observed, documented, and remarked on autogynephilic sexual arousal in females?

Wow... I'm hearing an empty, hollow echo in that department. Not one observation, study, or anything... oh wait, I hear some tiny voices outside the hall? Could it be? Why there ARE some folks saying that females do experience autogynephilia... but... what? Oh, yeah... that...

ALL of them are autogynephilic males who are claiming that their autogynephilia is the same as what women feel when they wear women's clothing... after all, wearing "sexy" panties gets them all going, so it must get women going too? Right? Ummmm no.

Seriously, where in the many thousands of diaries, autobiographies, and now online social media blogs published, is there ANY (credible, not catphishing by an autogynephilic male) female individual accounts of anything remotely like the autogynephilia so easily found in a minority of males? Seriously? Where are the copious accounts of how, when they were pre and early teens, that they became intensely sexually aroused upon trying on their big sister's bra and panties? Or looking in the mirror at their blossoming breasts and becoming intensely sexually aroused? Or examining their genitals and finding them so arousing that they masturbate while examining them... cause being female is just so sexy? No? Again that hollow echo.

Oh, but wait, I hear a rising chorus (of autogynephilic males) saying that a Dr. Charles Moser created an autogynephilic inventory for females and tested a group of women. So we ask, as we must assume the null hypothesis, where did he find the known autogynephilic females to interview to create a valid test? How did he validate it? What are the psychometric properties of the instrument? What? No? He did none of that? Well, then what did he do? He carefully rewrote questions from an instrument intended for and validated only for males in a gender clinic setting? Well, looking carefully at the rewrite, they don't seem to have even a passing bearing on what autogynephilia would theoretically look like in women, or even in androphilic transsexuals. The questions were very carefully written to get positive answers from heterosexual females, as that was the intended (political) goal, to "prove" that straight women were also autogynephilic... but they have no meaning. They don't measure autogynephilia, they measure mostly anticipatory arousal before dates with men. Well that was disappointing. One and only one demonstrably invalid study. We still have no evidence to disprove the null hypothesis. So, for now, we must accept that females do NOT experience autogynephilia.

OK, so now we know that autogynephilia exists in some males, but there's no (credible) evidence that it exists in females. But are there really two types of MTF transsexual? Does autogynephilia exist equally as much in exclusively androphilic transwomen? Let's assume the null hypothesis, that there is only one type, not two. We can use the previously developed and validated instruments to measure any putative autogynephilia in both exclusively androphilic and non-exclusively-androphilic transwomen and see if there is a difference. Here, we have a number of studies done over the years, Buhrich (1977), Freund (1982), Blanchard (1985), Doorn (1994),

Smith (2005), Lawrence (2005), and Nuttbrock (2009).

These studies all clearly indicate a strong correlation with non-exclusively androphilic reporting a high, nearly universal, percentage of individuals acknowledging autogynephilic arousal, either currently, or in early adolescence, and a strong anti-correlation with exclusive androphilia. Diving deeper, consider that in the largest and most recent of these studies by Nuttbrock (N=571), the grouping that had the highest percentage reporting sexual arousal to crossdressing was the gynephilic at 82%, while the group with the least non-exclusively androphilic was those who had begun Hormone Replacement Therapy (HRT) as teenagers, who had the lowest percentage reporting sexual arousal to cross-dressing at 14%.

To support the null hypothesis, there should have been no correlation with sexual orientation. The null hypothesis is NOT supported, there is NOT one group, but two. Further, the null hypothesis regarding autogynephilia not being correlated with gynephilic/bisexual/asexual transwomen, and only these transwomen, is not supported. Androphilic transwomen and natal female women do not experience autogynephilia.

But this only brings us back to where we started, with my correspondent fully conceding to the above. But she still has a valid question, does this mean causation? After all, we all know that correlation does not prove causation. But here we need to bring up a point, actually, it doesn't prove it... but causation does require correlation. So, we have our first step toward answering the question. With correlation, we may have causation. But we need to explore further.

One of the most accepted methods of deducing whether there is a cause and effect relationship in medicine, including psychiatric epidemiology, is found in Bradford Hill's Criteria.

The list of the criteria is as follows:

Strength (effect size): A small association does not mean that there is not a causal effect, though the larger the association, the more likely that it is causal.

Consistency (reproducibility): Consistent findings observed by different persons in different places with different samples strengthens the likelihood of an effect.

Specificity: Causation is likely if there is a very specific population at a specific site and disease with no other likely explanation. The more specific an association between a factor and an effect is, the bigger the probability of a causal relationship.

Temporality: The effect has to occur after the cause (and if there is an expected delay between the cause and expected effect, then the effect must occur after that delay).

Biological gradient: Greater exposure (dosage or intensity of cause) should generally lead to greater incidence of the effect. However, in some cases, the mere presence of the factor can trigger the effect. In other cases, an inverse proportion is observed: greater exposure leads to lower incidence (as found in vitamin deficiencies).

Plausibility: A plausible mechanism between cause and effect is helpful (but Hill noted that knowledge of the mechanism is limited by current knowledge).

Coherence: Coherence between epidemiological and laboratory findings increases the likelihood of an effect. However, Hill noted that "… lack of such [laboratory] evidence cannot nullify the epidemiological effect on associations".

Experiment: "Occasionally it is possible to appeal to experimental evidence".

Analogy: The effect of similar factors may be considered.

Taking each in turn:

Strength of the correlation is very high. Four out of five gynephilic transwomen acknowledge experiencing, currently or in the past, autogynephilia. Considering that autogynephilia is very rare in the general male population and non-existent in the female population, this correlation is very, very high. But it gets even higher when considering the experimental results of phallometry of those cross-dressers experiencing gender dysphoria who claim that they did not experience sexual arousal to cross-dressing, did in fact demonstrate mild sexual arousal to cross-dressing narration (autogynephilic erotic fiction) compared to control males.

Consistency of the correlation is easily shown by looking at the literature referenced above, in which study after study, over four decades, involving around a thousand transwomen, consistently shows the same data, even using different measures of sexual orientation and autogynephilia.

Specificity is shown in that it is only non-exclusively-androphilic males who experience autogynephilia and that a subset of those males develop gender dysphoria.

Temporality is demonstrated in that the majority of non-exclusively-androphilic males who become gender dysphoric and come to identify as women report autogynephilia in adolescence which seems to mellow even as their need to cross-dress and their gender dysphoria increases, reaching a threshold, a crisis point, most commonly in their mid-30's. As Prince (his/herself an autogynephile) and Doctor documented, "Among our subjects, 79% did not appear in public cross dressed prior to age 20; at that time, most of the subjects had already had several years of experience with cross dressing. The average number of years of practice with cross dressing prior to owning a full feminine outfit was 15. The average number of years of practice with cross dressing prior to adoption of a feminine name was 21. Again, we have factual evidence indicative of the considerable time required for the development of the cross-gender identity."

A **gradient effect** is easily found in autogynephilia in that men who have only very mild autogynephilia typically are content to cross-dress in private, never developing severe gender dysphoria or a female gender identity. There are individuals with partial autogynephilia who only wish to have breasts, who are content with mildly feminizing HRT, cross-dressing in public only occasionally. There are those who come to identify as "Bi-Gendered", "Gender Fluid", or "Non-Binary" who go back and forth. And finally, there are those whose autogynephilic ideation was intensely focused on being completely female and develop intense and all-consuming gender dysphoria who go on to live full-time as women, obtain HRT, and SRS. A number of studies have found that intensity and the specific nature of their autogynephilia correlates with these differential outcomes. Further, these effects seem to indicate both a continuum and a progression (criterion #4). There is another dosage effect that though subtle, is of high importance to the question of causation and the nature of autogynephilia itself found by Blanchard in "Nonmonotonic relation of autogynephilia and heterosexual attraction", from the abstract, "the highest levels of autogynephilia were observed at intermediate rather than high levels of heterosexual interest; that is, the function relating these variables took the form of an inverted U. This finding supports the hypothesis that autogynephilia is a misdirected type of heterosexual impulse, which arises in association with normal heterosexuality but also competes with it". This non-monotonic relationship was questioned in the Nuttbrock study, as they hypothesized that autogynephilia was a classic conditioned sexual fetish that had arisen as a consequence of cross-dressing and gender dysphoria, and not the cause.

But Lawrence easily demonstrated that Nuttbrock missed the relationship due to improper mathematical treatment of the data… and thus the dosage relationship evidence remains valid.

Plausibility. This is almost self-evident. If one's sexual ideation is exclusively autogynephilic, if each time such an individual sees herself as obligatorily female during sex, that would be strong drive towards gender dysphoria and an incentive to adopt a female gender identity, over time.

Coherence with laboratory tests are found by looking at brain sex research which shows that non-exclusively-androphilic transwomen are different from exclusively androphilic transwomen AND females, as expected by the theory that autogynephilia is the cause, not the result, of gender dysphoria and a female gender identity.

Experiments with animals are not possible as we have no animal models of autogynephilia.

Analogy is found in the amazing similarity of autogynephilia and its effects are found in males with apotemnophilia, the sexual desire for limb amputation, and autopedophilia, the sexual desire to be a child. In fact, a very high percentage of heterosexual apotemnophiliacs are also autogynephilic, experiencing an Erotic Target Location Error in which they wish to become female amputees.

So, we can see that we meet nearly all, saving only experimental evidence, to support the conclusion that autogynephilia is the cause, and not the result or merely a co-occurring factor, of gender dysphoria and female gender identity in non-exclusively-androphilic transwomen.

12 DIFFERENT MOTIVATIONS

The two types of transsexuals have very different lives, most notably different before transition, but even after for various reasons. They also have very different motivations, value systems, and decision making paths.

Dr. Anne Vitali, noted gender therapist, wrote several papers dealing with this sensitive subject. This brings up the matter of 'Identity Politics' in the larger 'Transgender' world. Language is important. I've often, "held my nose" as I used terminology in the papers I'm citing, so as not to confuse my reader. Here, Vitale has side-stepped the issue, by inventing de novo, just for the purposes of her papers, totally neutral language that is also completely non-descriptive and had it not been for her carefully describing the characteristics that define and contrast each type, we might not be able to compare her types with other authors. But here, I can provide that map. Her "Group One", as Vitale makes clear, consists of MTF homosexual transsexuals, while her Group Three are autogynephilic,

"Group One [MTF homosexual transsexuals] is best described as those natal males who have a high degree of cross-sexed gender identity. In these individuals, we can hypothesize that the prenatal androgenization process—if there was any at all—was minimal, leaving the default female identity intact. Furthermore, the expression of female identity of those individuals appears impossible or very difficult for them to conceal.

Group Two [FtM homosexual transsexuals] is composed of natal females who almost universally report a life-long history of rejecting female dress conventions along with, girls' toys and activities, and have a strong distaste for their female secondary sex characteristics. These individuals typically take full advantage of the social permissiveness allowed women in many societies to wear their hair short and dress in loose, gender-neutral clothing. These individuals rarely marry, preferring instead to partner with women who may or may not identify as lesbian. Group Two is the mirror image of Group One.

Group Three [autogynephilic transsexuals] is composed of natal males who identify as female but who act and appear normally male. ... They tend to live secretive lives, often making increasingly stronger attempts to convince themselves and others that they are male.

As a psychotherapist I have found female identified [MTF homosexual transsexual] males to be clinically similar to male-identified [FtM homosexual transsexual] females. That is, individuals in both groups have little or no compunction against openly presenting themselves as the other sex. Further, they make little or no effort to engage in what they feel for them would be wrong gendered social practices (i.e., the gender role assigned at birth as the basis of authority). Although I have seen some notable exceptions, especially in male-identified females, these individuals—at the time of presentation for treatment—are rarely married or have children, are rarely involved in the corporate or academic culture and are typically involved in the service industry at a blue- or pink-collar level. With little investment in trying to live as their assigned birth sex and with a lot of practice in living as closely as possible to their desired sex, these individuals report relatively low levels of anxiety about their dilemma. For those who decide transition is in their best interest, they accomplish the change with relatively little difficulty, particularly compared to Group Three, female-identified [autogynephilic] males.

The story is very different for Group Three. In the hope of ridding themselves of their dysphoria they tend to invest heavily in typical male activities. Being largely heterosexual, they marry and have children, hold advanced educational degrees and are involved at high levels of corporate and academic cultures. These are the invisible or cloistered gender dysphorics. They develop an aura of deep secrecy based on shame and risk of ridicule and their secret desire to be female is protected at all costs. The risk of being found out adds to the psychological and physiological pressures they experience. Transitioning from this deeply entrenched defensive position is very difficult. The irony here is that gender dysphoric symptoms appear to worsen in direct proportion to their self-enforced entrenchment in the male world. The further an individual gets from believing he can ever live as a female, the more acute and disruptive his dysphoria becomes"

The social consequences for the two types of MTF transsexuals is quite dissimilar. Before transition, Vitale's "Group One" [homosexual transsexual], is very visible, but becomes invisible after transition, while the opposite is true for her "Group Three" [autogynephilic transsexual],

> *"[homosexual transsexual] boys, who have a strong feminine core identity, typically develop a sexual interest in other boys during adolescence and prefer girls as peer friends. Although they still desire to be girls, they appear to have significantly less anxiety over not being female then that reported by the boys in Group Three. I believe this is due to the relatively uninhibited open expression of their femininity. For example Monica was 19 years old when she reported to my office accompanied by her mother. She wore gender-neutral clothing but otherwise presented as female in voice inflection and mannerisms. The problem, of course, was that Monica was genetically male. Monica's mother related to me that Monica had been more like a girl then a boy all her life. Her and her husband loved her dearly but thought of her more as a daughter then a son. Over the course of treating Monica, it became clear that although she was distressed over her male physiology, she was otherwise emotionally stable and very aware of the seriousness of her situation. Once it became clear that she was her own person and ready to undergo transition, a course of hormone replacement therapy was introduced. With the exception of having to face some extreme religious issues brought up by her much older brother, she accomplished an almost effortless transition from male to female. The presence of family support and little or no investment by the family or Monica in her being male made this transition straight forward."*

Vitale's use of the phrase "feminine core identity" harks back to earlier work showing that this type of transsexual has developed a female gender identity as a young child, while the other type, had not. She remarks that this type is very comfortable with their femininity and naturally find the idea of living as a girl to be agreeable. This is called "ego syntonic" behavior, as opposed to Group Three's "ego dystonic" behavior, where their desire to be female is unwelcome and out of step with their core identity as male. Note also the reference to Group One being "emotionally stable", making a tacit comparison to "Group Three", who, as Smith et al. put it,

> *"Homosexual transsexuals were found to be younger when applying for sex reassignment, reported a stronger cross-gender identity in childhood, had a more convincing cross-gender appearance, and functioned psychologically better than nonhomosexual transsexuals. ... The more vulnerable nonhomosexual transsexuals may particularly benefit from additional professional guidance before and/or during treatment."*

Returning to Vitale,

"To add to their confusion, and counter to behavior typically reported in openly gender dysphoric boys, many cloistered boys actually preferred solo play with boys' toys and had little or no interest in girls' toys. For example I have heard more than one long-time post-op male-to-female transsexual speak fondly of having spent countless hours playing with an Erector Set or a Lionel model train set-up that their father had helped them build. Others described designing and making detailed model airplanes, race cars and sailing ships. The more academic of this group report little or no interest in sports and rough and tumble play. To avoid castigation from their peers, they report spending a lot of time reading and studying. However, although these children appeared to be normal boys doing what most people would consider some normal boy activities, they may very well have been doing so while secretly wearing their mother's or sister's underwear, fantasizing about being a girl or both if they could manage it.

As sexual maturity advances, Group Three, cloistered gender dysphoric boys, often combine excessive masturbation (one individual reported masturbating up to 5 and even 6 times a day) with an increase in secret cross-dressing activity to release anxiety. In a post-op group I facilitated, Jenna (age 43) spoke fondly of the delight she experienced as a boy when she would find something of her mom's in the dirty clothes' hamper in the bathroom. Two others in the group laughingly agreed that they too took many a trip to the bathroom for the same reason. At the same time, in their public life, these boys report employing overtly stereotypical efforts to draw attention from their secret desires to be female by affecting appearances of being normally male. This includes dating girls, participating in individual sports activities such as swimming, running, golf, tennis, and for some, even body building.

Cloistered (Group Three) gender dysphoric boys appear to others and even to themselves to be heterosexual. Although as a group they are not especially active daters, they clearly prefer to date girls when they do date. Significantly, unlike other boys, their dating motives are markedly different. For these boys, being on a date with a girl is a chance to spend time with a girl in a way not generally allowed under other circumstances. Dating serves two purposes for these boys. The first is social, as it gives them the all-important appearance of being normal. The second is therapeutic. Being close to a girl's softness, and even her female smell, has a mitigating effect on gender expression deprivation anxiety. The fantasy is not to make love to her but to actually be her."

Note the rather direct description of use of female clothing as an aid to sexual arousal during masturbation. We have another name for this behavior, "autogynephilic erotic cross-dressing". Note also the reference to dating girls. Though she calls it "therapeutic", she is describing the phenomena of autogynephilia being simultaneously dependent upon and in competition with conventional gynephilia. Being with a girl has a "mitigating effect" on experiencing autogynephilic sexual frustration, which Vitale euphemistically refers to as "gender expression deprivation anxiety". This is remarkable, in that even in her own words, she clearly describes autogynephilia, *"The fantasy is not to make love to her but to actually be her"*. Very tellingly, as Vitale continues to describe older gender dysphoric individuals, her "Group One" simply disappears from her essay. This is because, by that age, they have either transitioned and become invisible or they don't ever transition. Simply put, there is no "late transitioning" "Group One" transsexual, while "Group Three" digs in and clings to their socially formed (core) male identity, while trying to ignore the cognitive dissonance created by their growing awareness of their autogynephilically enforced erotic ideal, their "desires to be female",

> *"As more information about transition to one's felt gender identity becomes available to the general public, we are seeing genetic males with strong core female identities and genetic females with strong core male gender identities present in their early twenties with the clear objective to being sexually reassigned.*
>
> *The cloistered, [autogynephilic] natal males, on the other hand typically start to realize the seriousness of their dilemma at this age. It is common to hear reports of these individuals increasing the intensity with which they try to rid themselves of the ever-increasing gender-related anxiety. Many individuals paradoxically adopt homophobic, transphobic, and overtly sexist attitudes in the hope that they will override their desires to be female."*

As she describes her "Group Three" as adults, we clearly see the pattern of late transitioning MTF transsexuals,

> *"For those who continue to struggle inwardly with their gender issues into mid-life, new issues come to the fore. As a time when most people realize that about half of life has been lived and feel the need to make an accounting of who they are and what they have done with their lives, this period can be especially anxiety provoking for the gender-dysphoric individual. Decades of trying to overcome an increasing gender expression deprivation anxiety begin to weigh heavily on the individual. Family and career are now as deeply rooted as they will ever be. The idea of starting over as a member of a different sex has become seemingly impossible. The fact that the need to change sex has increased rather than diminished, despite Herculean efforts, is now undeniable."*

Thus, we see clearly two mutually exclusive clinical patterns described by a veteran gender therapist. It is painfully obvious that there are two distinctly different types, with two different etiologies and life arcs. Blanchard's model of homosexual vs. autogynephilic transsexuality completely explains the clinical experience.

As was noted earlier, MTF homosexual transsexuals simply pass better, usually far better, than autogynephilic MTF transsexuals. We are still left with an open question. Why do homosexual transsexual transwomen pass so much better than autogynephilic? Three possible hypotheses exist, 1) Having a truly earlier age of onset and social transition age, they experience less masculinization from endogenous androgens. 2) Self-selection for passibility as they are motivated to fit into society better, being both physically and behaviorally extremely gender atypical (and not autogynephilically motivated). 3) Actually being, as a group, intrinsically more physically gender atypical. That is to say, that the etiological cause for their behavioral gender atypicality causes physical atypicality as well.

It's also quite possible that any or all of these may be operating. In fact, I strongly believe that all three are, in fact, operating. Homosexual transsexuals do transition and obtain cross sex hormones at an earlier age. They (we) do care and want to pass to better our lives. And, from research into gender atypical children, it has been noted that gender atypical and dysphoric male children are considered more attractive than their gender typical male peers. This 'attractiveness' is caused by hypomasculinity (masculine faces aren't "pretty").

Passing is multifactorial. How one looks, dresses, speaks, and moves all matter. One can do only so much with medical intervention. Even with breast implants and facial feminization surgery, someone with broad shoulders, narrow hips, large hands and feet, standing six feet four inches with a deep voice, lurching side to side as she walks is going to be "clocked", no matter how femininely dressed.

Back in the mid-90's, an out of town transactivist, a transwoman who had transitioned in mid-life, asked if she could visit my home, as she was passing through. I agreed and had her over for lunch. She arrived wearing a respectably skirted suit. She passed fairly well. Nothing about her looks or manner would have told most people that she was a transsexual. However, my then nine year old adopted daughter, Liz, insisted on using masculine pronouns. I was deeply embarrassed, mortified. I tried to correct her, but she angrily replied, "But he's a man!" with that look on her face that clearly said she thought I must be either blind or crazy. I've been told by many autogynephilic transsexuals that it can be very difficult to pass around prepubescent children, who always seem to read them instantly.

On another occasion, late at night, I got a call from a very distraught nineteen year old, pre-transition, pre-HRT, youngster that I knew as Stacey. She had had a fight with her folks and they had locked her out of the house. I'm sure you can guess what the fight had been about. For me, it was deja vu, having had the same one with my folks when I was seventeen. I drove out to her place and took her home. She was wearing a polo shirt and pressed slacks, boy's shoes. I put her to bed in our spare room. The next morning, Stacey had awoken early, gotten dressed in those same boy's clothes, and went downstairs to scrounge for breakfast. My daughter had gone downstairs before I had gotten dressed. She saw Stacey for a moment and, startled by a stranger in her house, ran back to me. She asked breathlessly, "Who's the girl in the kitchen?" I calmly replied, "Her name is Stacey…" My daughter rejoined Stacey and consistently, unreservedly, saw her as a girl, as they happily chatted together.

So, my daughter saw a post-op autogynephilic transwoman as a man, and a pre-transition, pre-hormone therapy homosexual transsexual as a girl!

Epilogue: A year or so after the events I described above, my lovely daughter was rummaging in my things when she chanced across some photographs of me as a small child, "Mommy, why are you dressed like a boy in these pictures?"

What was it about this polished older transwoman that led my daughter to attribute maleness to her in spite of her obviously female attire and appearance? What was it about Stacey that led my daughter to attribute femaleness to her in spite of her obviously male attire? What was it about me during my first weeks of high school that a strange boy should turn to another and ask in genuine confusion, "Is that a boy or a girl?" To which, the second boy simply shrugged.

The answer is likely sex-typed motor behaviors. Children are very aware of opposite sex typed motor behaviors starting at the age of five. That's also the age which many of the adult sex-typed motor behaviors begin to develop. This process continues into adolescence in a progression from sitting styles, to walking, to standing, to book carry. The female sex-typed book carry style, in which one uses the crook of one's arm and hip to support the weight is the last to develop.

Both children and adults can imitate some of the opposite sex type motor behaviors, but interestingly, not all. This is of extreme importance to passing, or rather the phenomena of being read or clocked as transsexual. It is widely understood that before transition, MTF "older transitioners" do not perform very many of the female sex typed behaviors naturally. But during the transition process, quickly learn to self-monitor and perform them. However, given that they can't continuously monitor their behavior 24/7, they are likely to relax when they feel in safer environments. But even when fully self-monitoring, as I feel certain my lunch guest was that day, she can't perform those female sex typed behaviors which most adult males can't perform. Some of these sex typed motor behaviors are so visible that I personally have been able to accurately clock an autogynephilic transsexual from the back, at up to 150 yards away!

On the other hand, MTF homosexual transsexuals perform many of these female typed motor behaviors naturally. As children, before transition, they may try to monitor and suppress these very behaviors that the autogynephilic transsexuals later have to learn to perform. Like the autogynephilic transsexual, but in the reversed gendered sense, there are certain behaviors that they can't control, can't keep from performing, likely due to their feminized brain. Thus, in high risk situations, such as in front of potentially aggressive boys at school, they may be taken for homosexual or even temporarily for girls. This can have negative consequences, even if overt violence is avoided. Gender atypical behavior causes most people to feel uncomfortable. This can lead to ostracism or lack of social cooperation. Thus, transkids suffer from lower grades, fewer social and job opportunities, and lower social status. After transition, these very same behaviors no longer need to be monitored, so for homosexual transsexuals, transition is both easier and actually increases their opportunities and status. Life is better after transition or they wouldn't do it.

But, for the poor autogynephilic transsexual woman, transition often reverses her social status and opportunities, often in subtle ways that she can't quite pin-point the cause. As one such transsexual put it to me years ago, "… before it was all smiles, now it's all frowns (from strangers)". The problem is even smiling is different in men and women as analysis has shown. Other times, loss of social status is direct and obvious, as Dr. Anne Vitale observed, these late transitioning autogynephilic transsexuals clearly understood that they would be losing their socially conferred straight male privilege should they transition,

> *"As the number of people who transition on the job grows, they get to see firsthand how public respect between men can quickly turn into private ridicule. Some individuals have even confessed to having participated in sexist jokes as a way to divert even the remotest suspicion from themselves. These people face the very real prospect of becoming outsiders, left to wither on the corporate vine. Given these seemingly unacceptable obstacles, many gender dysphoric males unconsciously accept certain male driven notions about women in an effort to purge the need to be female out of their mind."*

This typifies not only the different experiences, but the different motivations and decision making processes between autogynephilic and homosexual transsexuals.

In the late '90s, a transactivist friend cajoled me into attending the very last of the "New Womens' Conference" events. I was extremely reluctant to go for several reasons. First, I had no emotional desire nor need to attend a gathering I knew would likely be comprised of only "older transitioners", with whom I, save political interests, have nothing in common. In addition, one of the suggested activities was to bring dildos and share a group masturbatory session together. Fortunately, that was universally disapproved by all the rest of the conferees! I went because of my friendship, and the fact that she worked on my interest in trans-history research, and my love of being witness to such historic events.

During one of the sessions, Dr. Anne Lawrence, gathering research material, asked a forced choice question, "Would you rather be very beautiful, but unable to pass; or be plain but pass perfectly." Anne seemed very surprised at my very impassioned exposition on why I would choose passing. "One needs to pass to have a normal life. One does not need to be beautiful to find love. Lots of plain women find loving husbands." Looking around the room at the rest of the transwomen gathered there, all of whom were lesbian identified, I found no nodding of agreement, only uncomfortable silence. I don't want to sound narcissistic… and you can confirm for yourself by viewing my photograph on the back cover, that I both passed and was reasonably attractive… while the rest varied from 'could pass at the grocery store' to 'couldn't pass in the dark'. I very much doubted if any of the others were living as "stealth" as I was.

This difference is generalizable to all homosexual vs. autogynephilic transwomen. In my years of talking to other homosexual transsexuals, they universally would prefer to be 100% passable, even to being beautiful. Most of them were passable. Some were also beautiful. The need to be passible, and to actually pass, to live as stealthily as one can, is likely to be so important, as to be a major factor in the "transition/don't transition" decision making process. Bailey, in his book, *The Man Who Would Be Queen*, commented on this process, noting that it was indicative of a rational decision process whereby homosexual transsexuals made go/no go choices on which direction would lead to the greatest social success. But for autogynephilic transwomen, the ability to pass doesn't seem to enter into their decisions in the slightest.

The definition of "passing" seems to me to be different for homosexual and autogynephilic transsexuals as well. "Passing" for a large number of autogynephiles seems to consist of the ability to go shopping or to a restaurant without receiving rude comments. For the majority it does not seem to mean the ability to live in society for years, going to work, school, participating in civic affairs, visiting neighbors, all without any of them being aware, or even suspecting, of her transsexual status or history. Yet, for most homosexual transsexuals, this is passing. As one wrote on her own blog, passing for her is going out into the street at three a.m. due to a fire in the apartment building, no make-up, no padding, in an overly large T-shirt, and the firemen calling her "Miss". Anything less is not "passing".

Having stressed the importance of the ability to pass, I now have to explain that not all homosexual transsexuals do this well. Kiira Trea, in several of our lengthy correspondences, noted that socio-economic status (SES) seemed to be correlated with passibility. She advanced the hypothesis that as SES increased, the requirement that one be able to truly pass increased. She felt that homosexual transsexuals weighed their opportunities as girls against their opportunities as femmie gay boys.

As SES increases, the opportunities as femmie gay boys/men increase. One can go to college, study the arts, get a job in fields where being gay is less of a problem, and might even be a benefit, etc. While for low SES homosexual transsexuals, there are far fewer opportunities for them as femmie gay men and many more opportunities and less social disapproval, and even the chance for a normal and fulfilling life, as a woman. So, in the lower classes, those individuals who are on the edge of being transsexual vs. femmie gay man may be better off as a transsexuals. Thus explaining why we find more "in-betweenies" as Kiira called them, on the street. Kiira quipped that if one wanted to see an example of a truly passing homosexual transsexual, one needed to look to the upper-middle-class. (I should note, that I myself was raised as upper-middle-class, and after some difficulty in my early adult years, rose back to that level in my mid-to-late-20s.)

It has often been noted by clinicians and transsexuals alike that autogynephilic transsexuals will have had more highly paid, traditionally masculine, jobs before transition. For a mid-life candidate, transitioning successfully is expensive, what with electrolysis, hair transplants, tracheal shave, breast implants, facial feminization, and finally SRS. Further, losing straight male privilege may entail loss of opportunities for further career advancement, and likely losing a wife and children to divorce. Thus, I believe that there is a selection effect that occurs for autogynephilic transsexuals in that those who feel that they can "afford" it, are more likely to transition. We can see that in the clinically observed higher IQ in autogynephilic transsexuals. Intelligence is highly correlated with high Socio-Economic Status (SES). Thus, we can expect to find that autogynephilic transsexuals are more likely to have high SES… and the types of jobs that high SES men have.

Thus, we see opposite effects of socio-economic status in homosexual vs autogynephilic transsexual populations in that higher SES means fewer homosexuals and more autogynephiles.

13 PRE-ADOLESCENT GENDER ATYPICALITY & IDENTITY

In the 1960's, as transsexuality became more of a concern to doctors, they created a profile of what "true transsexuals" (homosexual transsexuals) were like as children. Some psychologists and psychiatrists then used this profile to gather male children who fit this profile. The most famous of these were Dr. Robert Stoller and Dr. Richard Green at the University of California Los Angeles (UCLA). However, their goal was not simply to study them, which they did, but to find ways to "cure" them before they became adult homosexual transsexuals, to "cure" them so that they would grow up to be conventional masculine heterosexual men. Their work was followed and emulated by numerous independent psychologists around the Western world.

This history has echoes in the present. There is an ongoing 'war of words' concerning the best course of treatment for gender atypical & dysphoric youth. Lately, as some in our society have learned to accept and even celebrate LGBT youth, there has been a reaction from religious and reactionary bigots who would wish to return to the days when parents and medical caregivers could treat gender atypicality as a serious psychiatric disorder that needed drastic interventions in and of itself, rather than a non-pathological variance found in all human societies. So, perhaps it's time to review the history of such interventions in the light of more recent scientific and humanitarian knowledge.

First, one must understand that historically, gender atypicality concerns were mostly focused on male children, 'sissies'. It was often assumed that 'tomboys' would outgrow it, but sissy boys would all too likely (and statistics bear this out) grow up to be homosexual or transsexual, both equally considered as disordered, criminal, and to be avoided at all costs. But in the 1960s, the doctors didn't know that most gender atypical males would grow up to be gay men, they assumed, because of the childhood histories of homosexual transsexuals, that all such extremely gender atypical boys would grow up to become homosexual transsexuals unless drastic interventions were taken.

To understand the nature of a given intervention one must first understand the underlying assumptions about the etiology of gender atypicality, dysphoria, gender identity, and sexual orientation that a given intervention was designed to address. During the mid-20th Century several competing theories vied with each other but there was a common thread, that of a disturbance of nurture. That is to say, that they rejected the role of biology and focused on the environment. So, if the environment is broken, so will the child be.

In this period psychoanalysis claimed illnesses were psychogenic that we now have clearly established as having neurological origins including schizophrenia and autism spectrum disorders. Typically, the quality of mothering was blamed. (Sound familiar?) Mothers were blamed for nearly every sort of bad outcome in their children, without ANY corroborating statistics or evidence. The ugliest of these was calling the mothers of autistic children, "refrigerator mothers", falsely accusing them of being emotionally cold and unavailable, and the mothers of schizophrenic young adults, "schizogenic mothers", falsely accused of being bad mothers, emotionally abusing their child such that they literally go crazy. From there, several theories about "emotionally disturbed children", children who act like the opposite sex, emerge; faulty family constellation, lack of "appropriate" role modeling, and the "Smother Mother".

The faulty family constellation theory is from observations that many children grow up in so-called "broken homes", where single mothers are raising children on their own, with no man in their lives. The theory is that a boy child simply has no male role model and thus learns only feminine behavior and identification. But, this wasn't true of all feminine boys. So, another term was added, the "emotionally absent" father. This was a man, who though physically present in the home, rejected his son and thus failed to mold the young boy's behavior toward the "healthy" masculine norm. Of course, a modern understanding would be that the boy's innate femininity had been the cause of the rejection by a homophobic father, not the other way around. Also, many masculine heterosexual boys had grown up in single mother households, so they had to add the term "vulnerable" to the description of the boys, that is to say, only those who were "vulnerable" to this absence developed into sissies.

Another theory also holds that the mother in these families tends to 'smother' a boy, hold him close to her body for excessively long periods, 'tie him to her apron strings', etc., such that he can't form a separate gender identity, or even any identity of his own, and thus "molly coddles" him to become a sissy boy.

Yet another theory held that the mother hates men, her own lack of social standing, and is angry and resentful of her son, so sabotages his self-identity and steers him to be a sissy out of spite.

To a modern scientifically based intellect, the creation and wide scale acceptance of such psychodynamic theories about the origins of both typical and atypical gender and sexual behavior seems incomprehensible. How could they ever even entertain such odd notions? But, if we understand that the ideas have at their core, the pre-Darwinian notion that humans are a special creation, unlike any other species on the planet, it starts to make some sense. While to us, the thought that gendered and sexual behavior comes from a mental process that, if we translated to our rodent cousins, would make it sound, and be, ludicrous: Baby rat sees Daddy rat's penis and notices she doesn't have one… and envies Daddy rat's penis… so she starts acting like Mommy rat to get Daddy rat's affectional attention, etc. But, if humans are a special creation, the theory doesn't have to work for our rodent, or even, or maybe especially (?) our primate cousins. These notions had their genesis in Late-Victorian Europe, which was then struggling with the implications of Darwin's theory of natural selection and evolution and spread to North America which is still struggling (!).

The intervention designed to 'fix' the faulty family constellation is to introduce a "healthy" masculine heterosexual male role model to the boy and encourage identification and subsequent modeling upon that man. Since it isn't always practical to require a single mother to find a suitable husband willing to take on the task of 'toughening up' the sissy boy, the goal is to place the boy in therapy sessions with a suitable role modeling therapist. For a pre-teen this would often mean "play therapy" with sex typed boys toys. Along with the play and modeling, the boy is "encouraged" to be masculine and to find enjoyment in being male. Ideally, there would also be family therapy where the boy's father would be encouraged to take a greater role in the child's upbringing and similar withdrawal of the mother's involvement. Playing with girl's toys is to be actively denied and punished, taking away beloved toys and dolls, often lampooned as "Drop the Barby" therapy. Another aspect would be to restrict the boy from having female friends and require them to participate in single sex activities such as scouting, etc. where they are often exposed to peer disapproval and even bullying, as a means of providing negative (aversive) "natural consequences" to their feminine demeanor. It sounds almost gentle and acceptable (compared to electro-shock or emetic drugs then in use in adult homosexuals). But underneath, the message to the child is that they are not "ok", that there is something deeply wrong with them, that they are not lovable as they are, leading to reduced self-esteem and increased loneliness.

While we can all applaud the idea of family intervention to encourage more paternal involvement and bonding, the idea of decreased maternal involvement is simply not justified given that we now know that the faulty family constellation theory is just plain bogus. Further, if a homophobic father can't step up and bond with a feminine boy, that boy will need his mother's acceptance all the more. Further, placing the blame upon the mother for having "encouraged" the boy's femininity in this manner is just plain evil.

Personal Note: At the age of ten, during the '67-'68 school year, I was sent to such "play therapy" with Dr. Peters (you can't make this stuff up), a tall bearded man in a large room filled with toys. I don't remember seeing any girl's toys in the room, ever. According to my parents, separately, since they divorced when I was a teen, I trust that they were both being candid with me; it had been the school psychologist who had insisted that I be referred to Dr. Peters and only Dr. Peters. This would also explain why my teachers interfered with my female friendships and forced me to interact with boys in class, and there was nothing subtle about it; why I was required to join the Scouts where I was hated, harassed, bullied, and eventually kicked out by the Scout Master, sneeringly, as "not Eagle Scout Material". — What I find saddening about the episode is that in my case, the faulty family constellation theory is completely reversed. My mother, though an amazingly capable and caring parent, was the one who became emotionally unavailable and rejecting. It was my good fortune that my Dad was always a very warm, loving, caring, and devoted father to all four of his children.

Another intervention that gained some currency in the mid to late 20th Century is, in effect, to place a child into a Skinner Box, that is to say, create a deliberate reward & punishment system, in therapy, in the home, and in the classroom, in which gender typical behavior is consistently recognized and rewarded, perhaps with tokens redeemable for desirable privileges, while gender atypical behavior is penalized by taking away tokens and even issuing infraction tokens. This type of therapy is based on the theory of behavior modification through operant conditioning. This type of environment is often used in cases of extremely "disturbed", aggressive, or violent children and teens where cooperative behavior is rewarded and aggression is penalized. Here, the theory is that the child is "gender disturbed", expanding the definition used for one class of children requiring extraordinarily harsh and controlling interventions to another. The researchers held a twisted notion of sex roles / gendered behavior as exclusively learned. That feminine boys were mistakenly learning behaviors that should by rights only performed by girls/women, calling them "talented mimics". There were a number of therapists / researchers who have published and recommended such interventions using just this pathologizing language.

One of these, George Rekers, a self-hating closeted gay man, a graduate student at UCLA under Dr. Green, not content to label gender atypical boys "disturbed", not satisfied with the stigmatizing term "effeminate" boy, coined the even more powerfully pathologizing and stigmatizing term "feminoid" in the manner of the racist stigmatizing of those with Down's Syndrome as "mongoloid". One of Reker's recommendations included abusively "spanking" (beating actually) young feminine boys when they committed some feminine behavioral infraction, often at the end of the day after counting up the infraction tokens.

Interestingly, Rekers own research showed that such feminine boys were essentially like gender typical girls,

"The amount of feminine play by the feminoid boys was found to be significantly greater than that of normal boys, but not significantly different from the predominantly feminine play patterns of the normal girls."

Imagine putting a gender typical girl through this? Yes, that's the moral and psychological equivalent. I can't even begin to express how evil I find this so-called "therapy". And this is what some parents and pundits wish us to resume?

As time went by, Dr. Green's subjects, even those who had not endured the programs various interventions, nearly all grew up to be gay or bisexual men. Only one out of a series of fifty feminine boys grew up to be transsexual. Dr. Green then realized and reported to the scientific community that the "sissy boy phenomena" was about future gay men, not universally about homosexual transsexuals.

Note the ratio, ~2% of these gender atypical kids "persisted" and later transitioned.

This brings us to the next issue, that of identifying which gender atypical children will persist as such and which will accommodate to the modern Western ideal of "straight looking - straight acting" gay men or "soft butch" lesbian women? As time went on, other clinics tightened their profile and studied a number of gender typical pre-teens, some, but not all of whom, showed varying degrees of gender dysphoria.

In one study conducted in the Netherlands, Steensma et al. found that of their pre-adolescents that 29 out of 53 subjects persisted as gender dysphoric and intended to socially and medically transition. That's ~55%, a big improvement in predicting which will grow up to be transsexual over Green's boys.

But, the more important data is that there is a difference between the ages of childhood assessment, the age at which their parents brought them to a clinic for evaluation. (The difference being on average a little over a year, or over 10% of their age, and a large effect size of d = 0.81) Why would the parents of persisters wait longer than those of desisters?

Because they don't! It wasn't that parents of persisters waited longer, it was that many desisters, desisted at an earlier age, such that their parents never brought their children in for assessment. As they get older, fewer and fewer parents of desisters would bring in their children. But, the persisters would continue to be brought in at later and later ages. Indeed, the authors specifically stated that from the interviews, the desisters clearly articulated that from age 10 to 13 were critical for their change in gender dysphoric feelings. While, for persisters, that same age only confirmed and strengthened their feelings. Thus, both the interview reports and the statistics agree that something special seems to be happening starting at around the age of ten or even a little younger,

> *"Starting around the age of 10, and for the subsequent years, the persisters indicated that their cross gender preferences and behaviour and their gender identity remained stable, but that their dysphoric feelings intensified. The intensification of gender dysphoria was attributed to three factors; (1) Certain changes in their social environment, (2) The anticipation of and/or actual physical changes during puberty, (3) The first experiences of falling in love and discovering their sexual orientation."*

The authors, in focusing on what the teenagers said were influential, may have missed a critical factor. What's so special about the age of ten? This is well before puberty. The authors focused on changing social factors, but could it be that biology is still the important factor? McClintock and Herdt point out that sexual attraction is first noted well before our classic definition of puberty, that of the maturation of the gonads and subsequent increase in testosterone, estrogen and progesterone. Instead, other hormones start earlier, typically around ten years old. And this is the age at which one's sexuality begins to be recognizable,

"With regard to sexual attraction, all persisters reported feeling exclusively attracted to persons of the same natal sex, which confirmed their gender identity as they viewed this attraction as a heterosexual attraction. They did not consider themselves homosexual or lesbian."

For the desisting boys, some came to recognize that they were gay or bisexual, essentially confirming the results of many other studies which have shown that gender atypicality in boys is highly correlated with homosexuality. However, a number of the boys self-identified as heterosexual, even though they also recognized some same sex attraction, that is, that they were bisexual.

For the girls, all of the desisters had become aware of the fact that they were heterosexually attracted to boys and wanted to be sexually attractive to boys. Thus, they were the classic tomboys who grow up to be straight women. But the persisting girls were all attracted to girls.

Thus, this study showed that the key difference between persisters and desisters among female bodied gender atypical / dysphoric individuals was sexual orientation, but among male bodied, it was not as clear cut, desisting boys were also androphilic or bisexual. However, what is clear is that persisting boys are all clearly unambiguously and exclusively androphilic.

The clearest finding is that whatever causes the process of gender dysphoria desistance, it is finished by the time a youth reaches puberty. If a youth who was clearly gender atypical AND gender dysphoric before puberty is still dysphoric at the age of puberty, they will almost certainly remain so for life.

In the last few years, Dr. Kristina Olsen and her colleagues in the United States have been conducting longitudinal studies of transkids. There are detractors who claim that social transition before puberty 'traps' desisters on a path toward being adult transsexuals, while others have strongly supported the idea that just as the 'real life test' separates those adults who are truly gender dysphoric from those that aren't, it serves just as well in kids. Well, the verdict is in,

"Children from our longitudinal cohort who would later transition were highly similar to transgender children (children who had already socially transitioned) and to control children of the gender to which they would eventually transition. Gender-nonconforming children who would not go on to transition were different from these groups. These results suggest that (a) social transitions may be predictable from gender identification and preferences and (b) gender identification and preferences may not meaningfully differ before and after social transitions."

One **can** predict which will persist and who won't. There are differences in identification and behavior between them. One can tell the difference between persisters and desisters and that social transition follows gender identity, not the other way around as some argue. Persisters take to social transition like ducks to water, while desisters do not. We've gone from 2%, to 55%, to nearly 100% over the last five decades.

Puberty Suppression (Blocking)

For physicians and other health care providers, an overriding concern is to "do no harm". One of the fears for such care providers is that of starting a course of treatment intended to treat a condition, only to discover that they misdiagnosed the patient and gave a treatment that not only was unneeded, but potentially harmful.

In the case of trankids, both MTF and FtM, the sooner one can begin hormonal treatment and social support interventions to allow them to successfully transition into the appropriate gender/sex role so as to take advantage of the normal adolescent physical and social maturation process alongside their peers, the better the long term outcome. It also helps to avoid the need for surgery or other painful and expensive interventions.

Because healthcare providers had not been able to accurately predict which gender atypical / dysphoric children will persist, a number of practitioners had begun recommending and using a puberty blocking protocol, under a harm reduction model in which the persisters are protected from the harmful effects of their endogenous hormones, while refraining from iatrogenic injury from exogenous cross-sex hormones in those who will desist from their earlier gender dysphoria. The current recommendation is that such puberty blockers be used until the individual is 16 or even 18 years old, at which time, if he/she is still a persister, they may be switched to cross-sex hormones, while the desisters may terminate the puberty blocking protocol at any time. There is a built in bias for desisters and against persisters in that desisters can begin a preferred hormonal protocol, simply by stopping the puberty blockers, but persisters must wait and "prove" to healthcare workers that they are ready.

The problem with this protocol is twofold. First, it is not without its own potential for iatrogenic harm in that delaying puberty too long reduces the eventual strength of the bones in adulthood. This may not be immediately harmful, but those children will someday be older adults, whose bones will be more prone to breaks. Second, for MTF transkids, delaying puberty means that they will continue to grow taller, potentially reducing their ability to pass successfully as female. This effect may however be welcomed by the FtM transkids.

Another problem with this protocol is that it is very expensive, far more expensive than cross-sex Hormone Replacement Therapy (HRT). For those who live in localities who do not have a generous state provided health plan or parents with employer provided insurance, this may be a deal breaker.

Another reason for using puberty blockers, never stated publicly, but probably just as, if not more, important as harm avoidance/reduction is that of political push-back. Prescribing cross-sex hormones to young teens raises too much reactionary transphobic opposition. Reversibly hitting the 'pause button' on puberty touted as giving transyouth more time to desist is an easier sell. But as we've seen, desisters do so before puberty. There is limited evidence that puberty blockers serve to give desisters more time. This fact has created another myth that is used by detractors.

The false meme that is used by opponents of prescribing puberty blockers is that, like social transition, it too, "traps" desisters on a path to become an adult transsexual (with the assumed value judgement that being a transsexual is a tragic outcome).

My snarky response to those who push this disinformation is, "Well - then we need to ban antibiotics because everyone who is prescribed them gets a bacterial infection."

14 A GOOD ENOUGH LIFE

Back in the early 1950s, as the Western public first became aware of transsexuality, most notably through press coverage of Christine Jorgensen in the U.S. and Roberta Cowell in the U.K., many were quick to note that "there is no such thing as a sex change", as though that proved something profoundly debunking. Well, this is both a true and yet misleading statement. It is true in that no surgery, then or now, can take a fertile individual of one sex and result in a fertile member of the other sex. What is misleading is that the goal of surgery was never fertility, but palliative. It is to allow individuals who suffer, and suffer greatly, from somatic gender dysphoria to inhabit a body that approximates that of the opposite sex to a close enough degree that it alleviates their dysphoria. Although many transsexuals would love to be fertile in their new gender, they are willing to accept this trade-off to enable a good enough life. The short hand for this process was "sex change". Stoller, in his 1968 book, *Sex And Gender*, described homosexual transsexuals as ardently wanting children including mothering, indeed bearing, infants,

> *"The ultimate progression for the [homosexual] transsexual ... has not yet been reached in our society: he would not only like to have is body appear completely female but he would like to have his internal organs so changed (for example, by transplants) that he would now have is own functioning ovaries and uterus, ultimately to bear a child truly his own."*

Stoller described a typical homosexual transsexual transwoman and concluded with, "The patient is now married and hopes to adopt children."

When I was first interviewed by Norman Fisk at the Stanford Gender Dysphoria Clinic as a 17 year old in early 1975, I told him of my hopes and dreams of finding a husband and adopting children. I recall telling him about how much I enjoyed the two summers I had spent as a swimming instructor teaching very young children and of the then previous summer employed as a nanny taking care of two boys, aged four and ten, from early morning to dinner-time. I had, of course, actively sought out babysitting jobs all through Jr. and Sr. high school, with a promise to all of my regular families that I would break any previous engagement for a job. I don't remember Fisk making fun of me.

In fact, at that very first meeting, Dr. Fisk recommended that I read Dr. Richard Green's book, *Gender Identity Conflict in Children and Adults*. In it Green wrote,

> *"The men who fall in love with and perhaps marry women who are themselves former males, by and large, have known their partners only as women. Their prior sexual experiences have been only with females. They consider themselves heterosexual and their relationships heterosexual. To varying degrees they are consciously and unconsciously aware of the biologic status of their partners, but it would be simplistic and would furthermore blur generally accepted definitions to call these men homosexual. Rather they are men who respond to the considerable femininity of male-to-female transsexuals, ignoring the dissonant cues of masculinity."*

Those very words, read when I was 17 years old, gave me hope that my dearest wish, to find and marry a straight man, hopefully to also adopt children, just might be possible, in spite of my own mother's words of encouragement that "No man will ever love you, you know." Fortunately, Dr. Green was right, and my mother was quite wrong. I've been married to a very kind, warm, and loving man for over two decades now and foster/adopted two girls. Bailey, in his book, *The Man Who Would Be Queen*, had a different view,

> *"Do transsexuals find partners? Certainly, homosexual transsexuals find sex partners after their surgery, but do they find steady partners? Do they get married? I have already mentioned my impression that homosexual transsexuals are not very successful at finding desirable men willing to commit to them. In part, this reflects the difficulty that men have with the notion of coupling with women who used to be men (no matter how attractive such women may be), as well as the difficulty most transsexuals have keeping their secret."*

So far, I could agree totally with Bailey. It is difficult, but not impossible, as Green documented decades before him. However, he goes on,

> *"But it also reflects the choices that homosexual transsexuals are prone to make. My impression is that they would rather have a relatively uncommitted relationship with a very attractive man than a committed relationship with a less desirable partner. Although the homosexual transsexuals I have met are all searching for "Mr. Right," perhaps in vain, their sex lives have all clearly improved after surgery. They can hide their past identities for a while, at least, and no longer have to worry about how to respond to attractive men who hit on them in bars."*

Bailey's experience was mostly with street kids, very low Socio-Economic-Status (SES) and insecure, chaotic, lives,

> *"They are outcasts as children because of their extreme femininity. They mostly come from poor, broken families, and family rejection is common. ... They have, in fact, had to cope with rejection and disapproval since childhood, because of their extreme femininity. And they have not had the advantages that tend to instill respect in the social order. The early chaotic backgrounds of so many homosexual transsexuals might help explain why they do not defeminize the way that most very feminine boys do. A feminine boy from a middle-class or upper-middle-class family has more motivation to "hang in there" until he normalizes his gender role behavior, because he has a good chance at a conventionally successful future."*

I've known plenty of homosexual transsexuals who would fit Bailey's observations, but then I've also known many middle and upper-middle-class homosexual transsexuals, especially those who had supportive families, who had stable lives, found loving husbands; and a few of them adopted or became step-moms.

Homosexual transsexuals can and do find a 'good enough life' after social transition; romance, family, career, home.

15 DETRANSITIONERS ARE NOT THE ENEMY

Detransitioners are not the enemy.

When I was 18 years old, on my own, effectively disowned by my family. (I say effectively, as I was given a meagre allowance with the stipulation that I was NOT to come home or be seen by any of the family's connections. That is to say, that I was treated as a "remittance man" for a while.) I was fully socially transitioned and was just beginning HRT. I had found a room to rent with kitchen and bathroom privileges. The owner, a young divorced mom with a young daughter and her twenty something brother lived downstairs. Two other women rented rooms upstairs. Oh… and they often had boyfriends spend the night… so this wasn't some female only space by any means. In fact, I even had a date with my land-lady's brother; we went to a Jr. College dance together. I couldn't really afford the rent, so I babysat the daughter in exchange to lower it to what I could afford. I should mention that I couldn't afford to eat either! I went hungry for weeks at a time. One of my high school friends found out about that and organized a food drive for me. I ate a lot of strange stuff from cans for a while! After several months of this… well, disaster struck. I got read and outed. No one in that house wanted a transsexual in the house, I was forced to leave.

So much for the theory that if people know an LGBT person, their hatred will be reduced; not in 1975 it didn't.

So, I had to find a new place, fast! I didn't have enough money to rent my own space, no matter how humble. I didn't know a single transsexual. I had never met a transsexual. I was completely alone, no community, no mentors, no one I could turn to. I can't properly express how lonely and afraid I was.

I was told about a place called the Alternative Community Center, where they had a bulletin board listing housing. I hoped that I could find an LGBT friendly space. I inquired at a good number of situations… While I found plenty of L friendly spaces, some G friendly spaces… there did NOT seem to be any T friendly spaces… In fact, in one mixed house I got quite the cold shoulder, openly hostile and vile comments. But as I walked out, one of the straight men, ran after me and excitedly talked to me, actually trying to flirt with me, then admitted he was a closeted cross-dresser (i.e. a gynandromorphophilic autogynephile)… and while he clearly wanted to be my buddy, he also wouldn't stick his neck out to support my joining the house-hold. I was becoming depressed and disparate. Then, my luck changed.

A very butch, tall, lith but muscular lesbian, had a room available in a rented house near the beach. She explained that it was temporary, it being winter, the off-season, so she had rented it fairly cheap. I could have the room dirt cheap. Her name was Curly Hummingbird. She was totally cool with me being transsexual. I couldn't believe my luck.

Living there was comforting and I felt more than welcome. Curly even set me up with a man she knew. She loved sharing with me that all her lesbian friends had the hots for me. She didn't tell them I was transsexual. She also made it VERY clear that she too found me attractive and would welcome intimacy.

As time went on, we had many late night discussions. It turned out that she was a detransitioner. She had lived for three years passing as a man. Yes, when gays, lesbians, and straights were all horribly transphobic when confronted by an actual transsexual, a detransitioner was my savior.

After several months, winter turned to springtime weather and the house rent went up. Curly was moving on (to live in a wymyn's land commune up in the Santa Cruz Mountains) and so must I.

I thought I had found a new savior, a mid-twenties, self-described "straight" transwoman I had met at the Stanford Clinic's "Grooming Seminar Series". She was very keen on me moving in with her. But she turned out to be a gynandromorphophilic sexual predator instead who one early morning demanded sexual favors or she would kick me out to be homeless again. I refused, she threatened violence; I was out the door that very morning. So, I learned that some transwomen could be just as dangerous as straight men, perhaps more so for being wolves in sheep's clothing.

But interestingly, at that "seminar", Dr. Laub, Sr., the surgeon of the clinic made an announcement that one of the popular members of that little community of autogynephilic transwomen had decided to detransition AFTER having SRS. This sent shock waves through most of the attendees, save for one twenty-something lesbian identified post-op who philosophized that "he" had found what he needed on his life's journey and that no one should feel sad about the situation.

Thus, the earliest lessons I learned in the transcommunity; detransitioning was real. It happened. It was not tragic. And they were not my enemy. Most detransitioners know the pain of gender dysphoria and fully support others following their best path to social success and happiness.

Detransitioners, people who actually socially transitioned for a length of time then later returned to living as their birth sex are actually very rare. Consider; as a percentage of those who have transitioned and, since transition itself is very rare, detransitioners are exceedingly rare. We know this from follow-up studies of those who have had medical interventions by clinics and other researchers. The numbers I've seen suggest that the rate, nearly all of which were autogynephiles (based on natal sex and age of transition), is only 0.2% . Consider, if only 10 people per 100,000 people transition and only two out of a thousand of those detransition; that means that there are only two in a million people who have transitioned and then detransitioned. Recall that there are only 325 million people in the United States. That would mean that there are only ~650 detransitioners, fewer than many high school student bodies.

I want to point out that someone who begins social transition and/or HRT but backs away from that in a short period of time should perhaps not be considered a detransitioner? After all, we have a consensus in the caregiving community that there should be a "Real Life Test" period sufficient to determine if such transition and medical interventions were the right thing for a given individual before irreversible interventions such as major surgery. Perhaps we need to view such as not being detransitioners so much as having conducted the medical / social / psychological tests and found that they were not right and count that as also a win? I've learned a new name for such folk, as they call themselves, "re-indentifier".

Remember those 'tucutes' falsely claiming "trans" identities I mentioned earlier? Many of them, as they get bored with that identity then claim to be either "re-identifiers" (a good thing) or "detransitioners" (not an accurate claim). How bad are the numbers being thrown around? I recently saw a claim that there were 13,000 "detrans" subscribers to a subreddit on the internet. Wait? What? When we see numbers like this being thrown around, we know that they can't all be actual detransitioners.

There is something else going on.

There is a behavior that is common in human societies of preferring those like themselves. In modern cant we call this tendency 'tribalism'. This extends to liking and preferring that people become more like themselves and believing that their way of life is better than others. This is the flip side of nearly all prejudice. This tendency means that if an out-group can't become like the in-group because of genetic / biological barriers like the color of one's skin or one's sex, then it leads to racism or sexism. However, if the difference can be (or simply perceived to be) merely one of lifestyle or choice, then it can develop into an insistence that members of the out-group must change their lifestyle or choices. If the difference develops from within an in-group to become a subgroup or to join an out-group, these individuals are considered 'traitors' to the in-group.

An example of this prejudice and its flip side is the need to convince others to either join in the in-group (e.g. religious evangelism) or to punish those who leave the in-group (e.g. death sentences for apostates).

Such is the experience of LGBT folk.

Homophobia is due in part to the anger and need to punish the 'traitorous' action of not being heterosexual, of becoming a member of a despised outgroup. This is why families can be the source of the most virulent hate that LGBT folk can experience.

This feeling of being betrayed and of loathing of those who fail to join or remain in the in-group is also part of transphobia, including by non-trans members of the gay, lesbian, and bisexual communities, in fact, especially by gay and lesbian people.

It is well-known now, and often uncomfortably recognized within the gay and lesbian community, that such gay and lesbians were quite gender atypical as children and many remain somewhat gender atypical as adults (excluding their gender atypical sexual orientation). To some, this recognition and memory of their own childhood before they accommodated to the Western ideal of gender typical acting Gay and Lesbian identities, they look to homosexual transsexuals and insist that they too accommodate to that same ideal, regardless of natural proclivities and desires. After all… they did. Quite literally, they see homosexual transsexuals in transition as traitors to the modern Western gay and lesbian identity, their tribe. And their tribe is best.

To these gay and lesbian tribalists, transkids who persist and transition are either victims of an imagined "transgender ideology" or are perverse 'sinners' against the true faith of Western Gay and Lesbian lifestyle. They are truly apostates whose voice must be silenced or devalued. On the flip side, desisters and detransitioners are seen as having 'seen the light of the true faith' and are upheld as proof that gender atypical children can escape, while persisters have been led astray by, that evil "transgender ideology". Some even carry banners at Pride events claiming that "transgender erases lesbians".

When I hear these claims, I can't help but hear another voice from another time that perhaps these gay and lesbian folks are too young to remember? I hear Anita Bryant and other homophobes of the late '70s calling to "Save Our Children", claiming that gays and lesbians are a danger to children and are "recruiting" otherwise "normal" children into the "homosexual lifestyle" which is part of the "homosexual agenda". I hear the exact same 'phobic lies but today it is from gays and lesbians and their hatred is poured out onto transfolk.

"transgender ideology" <=> "homosexual agenda"

If this seems like it is hyperbolic and specious, one only has to read the comments from many commentators, especially a certain subset of lesbians, that very specifically state that such "transgender ideology" has falsely convinced young gender atypical (i.e. butch) lesbians to believe that they must be transgender. They also insist that feminine MTF transkids should be taught that not only is OK to be a feminine man (never mind that modern Gay male culture is extremely femmiphobic and gay men won't be very accepting); that they should be gender atypical gay men and not transsexual, not transition to living as women.

That is to say, that this is seen as a cultural war between two tribal identities, two religious identities.

Another example of silencing or devalued is to portray the young transitioning homosexual transsexuals of Iran as doing so only to escape religious discrimination against gays and lesbians. Such discrimination exists, but the number of such transsexuals transitioning is on the same order as those transitioning in Thailand and FAR fewer than the number of gay and lesbian people in the general population. This false portrayal of "forced transition" is another example of tribalism using the specter of forced religious conversion coupled with the horror of unwanted body modification. But the truth is that these young people's lived experience is denied and their voices silenced, replaced by their own.

It has always amazed and irritated me that others who don't experience extreme gender dysphoria tend to tell persisters that it is all because of our false consciousness, patriarchy, internalized homophobia, misogyny, and/or 'transgender ideology'.

For a number of straight people, the plight of gender atypical and dysphoric children and teens is so alien to their understanding and experience that they quite literally can't see the world from the point of view of transkids. The ability to empathize, to place one's self into the shoes of another, is of utmost importance in life. Without it, we all would be sociopaths without a conscience, willing to allow untold suffering in others without making any effort to alleviate it. But because many people can't do that with transkids, they substitute an over-simplification of the Golden Rule… instead of treating others as those others would see us do, they treat transkids as they would like themselves to be treated. That is to say, instead of walking a mile in transkids shoes, they put their own shoes onto transkids; And when they see them in their imaginations, stumble with their ill-fitting shoes as their parents and caregivers attempt to help alleviate their dysphoria and lead a fulfilling life, cry,

"Child abuse!"

Thus, a certain subset of lesbians and transphobic straight allies are emotionally rewarding those young women, inviting them to join a new "cool kids club", those who renounce their prior self-identities as "transgender', encouraging them to call themselves "detransitioners", even though they never actually transitioned in the first place. These "detransitioners" are then weaponized as propaganda against affirming protocols for transkids.

Transsexuals Belong To The LGBT Community

As we saw, some gay and lesbian people do not appreciate transsexuals and argue that we don't belong in the same social and political coalitions. This is false.

Consider two recent issues fought and won in the Supreme Court of the United States; one on sex discrimination under Title VII; the other on marriage equality.

The battle for inclusion in Title VII should be a no brainer to understand. Transsexuality and sexual orientation are both about being discriminated "on account of sex", as the Court ruled.

Some LGB folk question whether marriage equality matters to the Transsexual communities, both autogynephilic and especially to homosexual transsexuals since if we are legally recognized as being in a heterosexual marriage, marriage equality didn't matter. But it does matter, because now our marriages will neither be invalidated nor our legal sex status put into jeopardy.

To understand, we need to review a little history.

When transsexual surgery and post-op legal recognition in the US first began, it was only for single people. In fact, the first transsexual person to be recognized in her new gender was likely Christine Jorgensen, who as a single person was able to get her passport amended after she had SRS overseas in 1953, so that she might return as legally female. Since then, it has been State Department policy to recognize a legal sex post-operatively. But what of married people?

When SRS was first offered legally in the US, at a limited number of medical clinics, it was no secret that they struggled to understand who was a valid candidate. Most of the clinics refused to offer services to those that they understood to be heterosexual transvestites, autogynephiles. And they used a current status of being married to the opposite biological sex as one such indicator. Further, these clinics were loath to artificially create "homosexuals" out of straight people. Some of this was because of internalized heteronormative values, some of it was genuine fear of legal liability. After all, if one performs what was then considered "experimental" SRS on a husband, would not the wife have legal grounds to sue due to estrangement and denial of conjugal rights? Since same sex marriages were not valid, would not their marriage also be adjudicated invalid if their husband was now legally female? Or would the courts refuse to recognize the change of sex and thus enforce the marriage? The clinics wanted nothing to do with this potential legal mess, so refused to perform SRS on married people. So, many candidates for SRS back in the '70s got divorced, even when they remained on good terms with their female partners, just to secure SRS.

A bit of personal history. Back to 1976. I remember well the irony of sitting in a room full of autogynephilic clients at the Stanford Gender Dysphoria Clinic, listening to a lecture from a lawyer telling the room about how to ensure that their future marriages, which he presumed to be with men when we became post-op, would be "valid". Truly, I was the ONLY one in that room that cared for his advice! The rest wanted to know how to KEEP their present marriages to women valid ! Unlike many clinics, Stanford did NOT discriminate against gynephilic and admitted autogynephilic transwomen. Thus, the burning question on their minds was, would the law still recognize them as married and simultaneously female after SRS? Though Stanford didn't discriminate against autogynephilic transwomen, it did insist that they be unmarried at the time of SRS.

In a sense, the question was never adjudicated, to my knowledge, for transwomen married to women. But marriage and recognition of legal sex

DID become an issue for a fair number of homosexual transsexuals married to men… sometimes with a positive outcome for both questions, and sometimes with a negative outcome for both questions, depending on the State and the court.

Here is how it gets personal. I've been legally married in the State of California for over two decades. I love my husband very much, and with or without legal recognition, I would still be with him and consider myself his wife. But I wanted and still want our marriage to be valid and recognized. And therein lay the rub. I was born in the State of Texas, which at the time we were married, did NOT recognize either "sex change" nor post-operative transsexual persons' marriages. Texas would not change a birth certificate for "sex change"… but that didn't stop me from getting a "corrected" one, to correct the "clerical error" of the wrong name and sex, oopsie! So, in the State of Texas, should the court have discovered my subterfuge, a Texas court would likely have declared me legally male and my marriage void, (as happened to Christine Littleton around that time). I vowed never to live in Texas!

It should be noted that Texas has since changed its policy on transsexual birth certificates and a Texas court has since reversed precedent and declared that transsexual persons marriages to their spouses of the opposite (legally recognized) sex to be valid. Further, since California Prop. 8 was declared unconstitutional and same sex marriage is recognized, followed by the 2015 on national marriage equality my marriage is just that much more protected from court challenge.

But there are still countries and courts where this is not clear. But if an MTF homosexual transsexual's marriage can't be voided by declaring her legally male, 'phobic judges will have less incentive to do so. And similarly for an FtM transman married to his wife. So it still matters to homosexual transsexuals that the legislatures and courts decide that same sex marriages are the law of the land. And it matters even more to autogynephilic transwomen still, or wishing to be, married to their female (or even other transwomen) partners; that their marriage status is both legally secure and is no longer a concern to medical providers.

16 THE GREAT CONFLATION

There's always the question, how and why did the two types of transsexuals, if they are so obviously different, become so conflated and treated with the same protocols? For that, we need to review a bit of history.

In the May 1974 issue of the *Western Journal of Medicine*, two back to back articles appeared, one from a number of doctors reporting on a grand rounds at UCSD hospital that included Robert J. Stoller and one from Norman M. Fisk. Reading them both now is not only a window on the past, but explains where we are now and how we got here.

I can't write about this period without flashing back on my own life and what was happening at the time. In May of '74, I was 16, just about to turn 17, finishing my junior year in high school. My favorite class was "Individual Voice", solo singing, but I was also really enjoying one other class, "Cosmology; Stellar and Galactic Evolution" I was taking at a local community college, taught by a NASA astronomer. I got an "A" in the class, of course. I was also summer job hunting and landed my dream job as a nanny taking care of two boys for a local family for $50 a week (~$250 in today's money – a fabulous sum for a teenager back then). I was also desperately searching at the library for any and all information I could find on transsexuality and how I could get hormones and surgery. That search led me to the Stanford Gender Dysphoria Clinic and Dr. Fisk.

In the fall of '74, I contacted the clinic but was told that since I was legally a minor, I had to have my parents' permission.

In early '75, after much drama with my parents, who were separated and soon to be divorced, I finally convinced them to let me go to the clinic (but failed to mention that they performed sex reassignment surgery, etc.), which meant first being evaluated by Dr. Fisk. During the early part of the first interview, I got the very distinct impression that he didn't believe a word I said, though it was all the absolute truth. From his article, we can see why,

> *"The concept of gender dysphoria syndrome grew out of clinical necessity very much in an organic, naturalistic fashion. This occurred because virtually all patients who initially presented for screening provided us with a totally pat psychobiography which seemed almost to be well rehearsed or prepared, particularly in the salients pertaining to differential diagnoses. It would be accurate to say that of the initial 30 to 40 non-psychotic patients screened, all presented as virtual textbook cases of classical transsexualism. Remembering the old medical saw that "the last time one sees a textbook case is when one closes the textbook," it was apparent that this group of patients were so intent upon obtaining sex conversion operations that they had availed themselves of the germane literature and had successfully prepared themselves to pass initial screening. In some instances they had rehearsed friends, spouses and family members in a similar fashion."*

During a later interview, in the company of my mother, who with obvious disapprobation and the mistaken notion that the clinic was to "cure" me, answered his questions about my early childhood saying,

> *"He was very different than his brothers. All of their friends were boys, his were all girls. ... He was very prissy. I could dress him in clean clothes on Monday and they would still be clean on Friday. ... I've known he wanted to live as a girl for years. I just felt that was wrong."*

In the next interview, in company with my father, who tried to argue with him about what should be done about me after learning that I had been diagnosed as transsexual, Dr. Fisk replied,

> ***"Denial will not serve. You will win some battles but lose the war."***

That made Dr. Fisk my hero for life! And he should be a hero to every autogynephilic transsexual who has come after, since it is Dr. Fisk who changed the way transsexual people are treated that continues today,

> *"Within the first two to three years of our investigation, it became apparent that when non-fabricated or, more precisely, honest and candid*

psychobiographies were obtained from our patient population, there was indeed a great deal of diversity and deviance from what had been defined as the symptoms of "classical transsexualism." Moreover, the overtly present common denominator was the high level of dysphoria concerning the individual's gender of assignment or rearing ... employing the diagnostic term gender dysphoria syndrome, our indications for surgical sex conversion therapy have been broadened. Patients now clearly understand that had they been interviewed five or ten or twenty years ago, they would have been diagnosed as not being classical transsexuals. These patients are informed that a diagnosis of transsexualism is not in our view the only valid criterion for deciding who receives surgical sex conversion. Moreover, we practice the rather pragmatic dictum that nothing succeeds quite like success and therefore our criteria for surgical sex reassignment or conversion are more phenomenologically oriented. ... Obviously, by liberalizing the indications for sex conversion through conceptualizing patients as having gender dysphoria, we also are committed to provide a program for patients encompassing many factors related to a total overall rehabilitative experience. These include vocational counseling and guidance, psychological and psychiatric supportive therapy, grooming clinics where role-appropriate behaviors are taught, explained and practiced, legal assistance, and, probably of most benefit, an opportunity is afforded to meet and interact with other patients who have successfully negotiated gender reorientation or who are in various phases of reorientation. This program employs some former patients as counselors to persons with gender disorders."

While Fisk's liberalization had eliminated the absolute need for a differential diagnoses for purposes of determining who was to receive services, in the long term, over the decades since, it has led to a false belief within the public perception that there are no differences on the one hand and to the harmful homogenization of treatment protocols on the other. It is important to note that the Stanford clinic did know that there were in fact two types and organized their services around helping those most in need of "gender reorientation": autogynephiles.

Having seen the best of times... we now turn to the worst of times.

During that psychiatric grand rounds at a UCSD hospital, a 20 year old MTF homosexual transsexual was paraded in front of a large group. The author of the May '74 article describing the event used masculine pronouns to introduce her to his readers and give a bit of her history, then switched to feminine pronouns. Here's an excerpt,

"She was told that this interview would be part of a training session on transsexualism so that people in the Department of Psychiatry could learn more about it. She was also told that this session will have no bearing on her

treatment, continuing evaluation, or the decision regarding her operation. She understands that coming here is entirely voluntary. (The patient, whom we shall call Gloria, was escorted into the room. She wore women's clothing, was heavily made up, and quite attractive. She was introduced to Dr. Parzen, who interviewed her before a group of approximately 100 staff members and residents.)"

Does anyone today believe that "Gloria" didn't fully understand that her voluntary cooperation was actually mandatory if she was to successfully navigate this clinic's hoops? Certainly she did given the times, as Dr. Parzen says,

"These patients become good actors and tend to be paranoid toward anyone who might push them to betray themselves in a way that might jeopardize their surgical treatment. Gloria had already established a personal relationship with Dr. Millman, and his feelings about her will ultimately determine what will happen to her."

The doctors had ultimate power of granting or denying services and transsexuals knew it! What's interesting is that the doctors knew that they knew it, but saw nothing wrong with this imbalance of power save for complaining about what transsexuals do in the face of such asymmetric power,

"Certainly she is quite protective about herself at this point. She is awfully close to getting what she wants, and she isn't going to tell me anything that might interfere with that. She does not know my orientation, and she isn't crazy, and therefore isn't going to present material that might be interpreted wrongly from her point of view. Transsexual patients classically tend to be very manipulative and very secretive. They tell you what they want you to know, and they have learned through much experience to read and to manipulate medical staff."

I could go on with the odd ideation that these physicians have that relied on classical Freudian psychoanalysis, not to mention the incredibly disrespectful things these doctors said about "Gloria" and transsexual people in general.

Just a few years later, in 1978, at the Harry Benjamin Gender Dysphoria Symposium, held at Stanford University, Richard Green, M.D., expounded on the problem of the age,

"The name of the game is follow-up. The controversial question of the

early 1960's: "Should transsexual surgery be performed?" has metamorphosed into the compelling question of the 1970's: "On whom should it be performed? '~ Various viewpoints exist regarding the appropriate candidate for sex-reassignment surgery. It has become increasingly clear that candidates cluster into three major groups: 1) individuals who report a lifelong core-morphologic sexual identity contradictory to anatomy, an absence of effective socialization in the role expected by virtue of their anatomy, an absence of genital arousal accompanying the wearing of clothes of the other sex, and an absence of genital pleasuring with partners of the other anatomic sex ("true transsexuals"); 2) males who have vacillated in their sexual identity or have been ambivalent in their identity from childhood, who have experienced genital arousal accompanying cross-dressing and who have had sexual relationships with persons of the other sex ("transvestic transsexuals"); and 3) individuals whose core-morphologic identity has been primarily consistent with anatomy, who have manifested gender-role behavior that is culturally atypical~ who have not experienced sexually arousing cross-dressing, and who have had extensive sexual relationships with same sex partners ("feminine male and masculine female homosexual transsexuals"). Some eventually receive surgery; others do not."

Green wanted to answer this burning question, just who would and would not be helped by transition and SRS. Transsexuals were notorious for disappearing after they got what they wanted out of the surgeons, so follow-up studies tended to be skewed to those segments of the population who would be inclined to cooperate: those needing constant validation. Green proposed that transsexuals be required to post a substantial bond to get service. That bond would only be returned in tranches as they came back for follow-up.

"I propose the following: Each individual who is accepted into an evaluation program for sex reassignment surgery must deposit an appropriate amount of funds for the anticipated professional services into a follow-up, interest-bearing, escrow account. In the case of medically indigent patients, the State or some third party should deposit a comparable amount on the patient's behalf. This money is to be returned to the patient at bi-annual visits over a ten year period, one-fifth of the total amount at each visit."

This would in effect raise the hurdle that less affluent, younger transsexuals would have to clear. I can tell you from personal experience that this would have had the effect of driving yet more transkids onto the streets, into sordid means, or to using the services of underground butchers like the infamous Dr. Brown in California. I could well imagine that for well-to-do older transitioning folk, the bond would represent an affront, and may even backfire, causing less cooperation rather than more. Fortunately, this proposal went nowhere.

But the question still remained and in his opening statement, Green shows us a murky problem for the clinicians. Just who was a "transsexual"? On one side, they could clearly recognize transvestites, men who clearly were or had been sexually aroused by cross-dressing. On the other side, they could clearly recognize homosexual men who occasionally put on drag to go to clubs, or homosexual women, who presented as butch as our culture allows. And they believed that they saw a group in the middle, who requested somatic feminization or masculinization, to allow them to live as members of the opposite sex. So far, pretty straight forward. But what to make of those folks who requested such somatic changes, but could be recognized to have very strong resemblance to transvestites or homosexuals? What of those who, in their presentation and narratives, downplayed such resemblance, but hints were there anyways?

The problem some thought was to find those bright shining lines that served as a demarcator for being a "true transsexual", to separate those who were actually either homosexual or transvestite, calling them "pseudo-transsexuals". Some researchers already thought that they had found these bright shining lines.

Person and Oversey had simple, bright shining lines for MTF types. If you were attracted to men, you were homosexual, period. If you were having, or ever had, sex with women and cross-dressed, you were a transvestite, period. Their "primary transsexual" was completely asexual, but had vacillated on their gender identity growing up, usually having made "one last effort to be a man" before succumbing to their disorder. They readily admitted this was a very tiny minority. (Blanchard later demonstrated that Oversey & Person's "primary transsexual" was autogynephilic.)

Green's description of the three types is recognizably based on Stoller's typology of "true" or "primary" transsexual. For MTF, his bright shining lines were drawn very tightly. If you were attracted to men, but used your penis, you were a homosexual, period. If you were attracted to women, and/or experienced arousal when cross-dressed, you were a transvestite, period.

Notice that Stoller's and Person & Oversey's "primary transsexual" were mutually exclusive, they didn't even overlap!

Even Fisk at Stanford, which had the most liberal policy for acceptance for SRS, used a tripartite model: homosexual, transsexual, transvestite.

Using these indicia, various clinics made decisions as to who they would deign to allow SRS. Different clinics had different criteria, ranging from strictly "true transsexuals only" to very liberal, everyone welcome, so long as you pass the "Real Life Test" (successfully passing for some period of time). Of course, you could always go overseas or Mexico, where if you had the money, they had the knife!

Given these models in use by various programs, there was a powerful incentive to lie, to craft one's personal narrative and history to fit the acceptance criteria, as stated by Berger, as reported by Green,

> *"It certainly seems that we are all agreed that one of the problems that we are trying to deal with in evaluating results is determining what happens to these people postoperatively. I think that it is equally a problem in that we do not know what happens to those who are rejected. I think that these people are consummate actors in many cases, and that when they are rejected, they learn what it was that they said wrong so that they can go to the next place and say it right. Since we do not communicate with each other and have no way of doing so about our results with specific patients, there is no way that we can really follow up a specific patient in their travelings from clinic to clinic."*

This lying became very extensive, as Deidre (Donald) McCloskey, whose 1999 autobiography *Crossing: A Memoir* documents numerous episodes of auto-erotic transvestism, writes (using the third person "Dee"),

> *"The young woman psychiatrist asked Dee the usual questions, mentally running down a checklist of the gender-crossing illness. "When did you first want to be female?" "Were you effeminate as a child?" (…) Dee started to lie. They all do it. Of course gender crossers lie. They can read the DSM just as well as the psychiatrists can. "Oh yes" Dee said to the Free University psychiatrist, "I've always had these desires. Oh yes Doctor ever since I can remember. Oh yes it's **just** like being a woman in a man's body. Oh yes Doctor I **hate** my penis. Oh yes Doctor **whatever your dopey list says.**"* (Bolded text is as originally printed)

Note that McCloskey's interviewer is asking questions based on Stoller's "true" transsexual profile which is a very accurate description of MTF homosexual transsexuals. This lying has distorted research, paradoxically adding weight to what we later learned was a flawed concept, to wit, that autogynephiles were poor surgical candidates. But as Berger shows above, and Meyer shows below, the fact that SRS candidates lied was very well known.

> *"It should be borne in mind that there is a degree of uncertainty in the data. This uncertainty derives, among other factors, from having seen the patients intermittently, rather than continuously, the patients' tendency to dissimulate in order to achieve sex reassignment, and the confidentiality of the evaluations which prevented direct checking of statements. … However, since most patients are aware from the literature of the "correct" early history, a degree of common falsification, and therefore factitious similarity, must not be discounted."*

In contrast to this concept of the bright shining line, was the continuum of symptomology and gender dysphoria. Harry Benjamin himself thought this was true. Meyer at Hopkins held this opinion. He clearly described a range of autogynephilic and separately homosexual individuals who requested SRS. Interestingly, he also described a group he called "Eonists", which I recognize as transkids, both MTF and FtM. (Ironically, he used the term "Eonist" which was named after a famous historically significant cross-dresser, who by his history, is easily recognizably autogynephilic.)

So, as Meyer and Benjamin described, Freund pointed out, Blanchard powerfully demonstrated & defined, and Nuttbrock recently corroborated (if unwillingly); there are no bright shining lines dividing and creating a middle group. There is nothing between the classic extremely gender dysphoric autogynephilic transsexual and the classic closeted transvestite. There is nothing, save possibly social status and opportunities, between the classic demure "true transsexual" and feminine gay men. There is only one line, the one separating homosexual from autogynephilic transsexuals. But that is not the line that may be used to determine who is and who is not suitable for somatic feminization.

In the end, I think Meyer summed it all up best,

> *"One is faced, however, with more ambiguity than clarity when the differential diagnosis for applicants requesting sex reassignment is limited to homosexuality, transvestism, and transsexualism. Far too many patients fall into the gray areas between. The selection of an overall classification, with the addition of descriptive subcategories, would seem more workable.*
>
> *With this in mind, I would propose recognizing the condition of sufficient gender discomfort, skew, or unease to request sex reassignment as the "gender dysphoria syndrome." This admirable term and its application, to my knowledge, were originally suggested by Norman Fisk (1973). As mentioned previously, factors in assigning the "gender dysphoria syndrome" label would be a sense of inappropriateness or incapacity in the anatomically congruent sex role, a sense that improvement would ensue with role reversal, … …and an active desire for surgical intervention. Explicit in this definition is that the*

patient take some active steps to realize the interest in reassignment. … The use of "gender dysphoria syndrome" has the added advantage of emphasizing disharmony within the patient's own gender rather than implying, as in the term "transsexualism," the successful negotiation of a gender, even though an anatomically incongruent one.

There is still the question of how to deal with the loosely used, generic term "transsexualism." I find that I can no longer use "transsexual" or "transsexualism" without quotation marks. The use of this term suggests that there is a single diagnostic entity "transsexual," which in current loose usage is characterized by a request for sex reassignment. All applicants, however, are not the same, and reassignees from the various clinical categories will presumably react quite differently to their surgical modification over time. Kubie and Mackie (1968) have previously emphasized these problems of definition as they relate to follow-up. An appreciation of the presenting clinical varieties emphasizes the need for great specificity in initial patient characterization if one is to speak of improvement or deterioration over long-term follow-up. Without these preliminary distinctions, with all patients lumped together, the truly valuable information will wash out of follow-up series and any opportunity for specificity in future prognosis or selection will be lost.

I would propose that the term "transsexual" be abandoned except for one specific usage. The term should be reserved only for those patients who have actually undergone, and completed, genital reassignment. The term, therefore, would refer to an anatomical fait accompli, and would have no further meaning. It could then be used as a purely descriptive term without implications regarding etiology, psychodynamics, character structure, preoperative adjustment, postoperative course, etc. It could be used much as the term "amputee" to describe a postoperative fact, with no implication as to physiological dynamics (diabetes, arteriosclerosis), character structure (alcoholic, drug addict), or the hazards of the fates (accidental trauma)."

Blanchard disagreed with Meyer and thought that it was not useful, nor particularly definitive, to use genital surgery as the demarcator for being 'transsexual', instead choosing to define them as those who were both gender dysphoric and sought social and medical transition services. I couldn't agree more! After all, many FtM transsexuals forgo genital surgery as current procedures are both prohibitively expensive and not always satisfactory, while transkids may be years from being eligible for surgery.

The clinics were very aware that there were two essential categories of transsexual and eventually were willing to accommodate their needs, although they didn't have a theoretical underpinning to that recognition.

However, these clinics tailored their program's requirements to the needs of the overwhelming majority, which were autogynephilic. The rules, or "hoops" as they were called by the prospective clients, were felt to be primarily designed to legally protect the physicians from malpractice lawsuits should there be post-operative regret. They were also seen as deflecting legal concern about performing "experimental" surgery that many in society thought to be immoral. The least popular "hoop" was the so called "Real Life Test" (RLT), the requirement that a prospective client had to live full time as a woman for some period of time, varying from six months to two years, depending on the clinic, before surgery could be obtained. For autogynephilic transsexuals for whom obtaining surgery was their highest goal, this requirement was felt to be unnecessarily onerous and even further proof that the clinics were restricting surgery to homosexual transsexuals. For the older autogynephilic transsexual who had likely struggled, attempting to suppress her desire for somatic feminization, and now come to embrace this desire, this further, externally imposed delay, was most unwelcome. Many clinicians remarked on the impatience and anger of these "secondary" transsexuals to this delay. One such individual angrily remarked to a group of transsexuals at the Stanford clinic, "They only want to do surgery on secretaries and prostitutes!" alluding to the two most stereotypical occupations of young homosexual transsexuals (personal recollection - I was a 19 year old secretary at the time).

The real purpose of the RLT was indeed to reduce the chance of post-operative regret from what was then considered "secondary" transsexuals, about which many clinicians remained uncertain that SRS was a useful treatment. Due to limited financial means, young homosexual transsexuals were rarely in a position to pay for surgery until they were older, most often many years later than any clinically imposed delay. For these kids, transition and hormones alone were both welcome and financially expedient. The older homosexual transsexual was likely to have been living as a woman for years, with no help from clinics, having obtained prescriptions for hormones from urban physicians familiar only with homosexual transsexuals that were referred from others. For an MTF homosexual transsexual, living full time as a woman is not a "test", but simply getting on with life. So the "Real Life Test" requirement was indeed literally instituted for the older autogynephilic transsexual client alone.

These clinical practices formed the basis of what would later become the Harry Benjamin Gender Dysphoria Association (HBGIDA, now renamed WPATH) Standards of Care (SOC) when that organization was formed in the late '70s. The existence of the clinics and the formation of HBGIDA sowed the seeds of the present boutique medical care system of independent gender therapists, private primary care physicians prescribing hormones, and independent surgeons. The availability of independent surgeons in turn led to the demise of the majority of the university based research clinics, as the boutique system was more convenient and lower cost. With their demise the SOCs were locked into place, institutionalizing one-size-fits-all protocols suitable for adult autogynephilic transsexuals, but totally inappropriate for homosexual transsexuals, most of whom present as teenagers or very soon thereafter. Also lost with the demise of the clinics was the institutional recognition of the very existence of homosexual vs. autogynephilic transsexuals by the majority of gender therapists. Thus, the needs of homosexual transsexuals had been made invisible.

In spite of the liberalization of the selection criteria, indeed the elimination of all criteria save passing the RLT, the lying, the distortions in sexual and gendered history continues, both to clinicians, therapists, and the public, most especially about one's sexual orientation, partially due to pseudo-androphilia.

For example, a 2014 study by Auer et al. it suggests that five of the eighteen putatively originally androphilic transwomen had changed their sexual orientation to bisexual, gynephilic, or "unknown". I have another interpretation: These five individuals simply admitted to actually having always been non-exclusively-androphilic, finally acknowledging it, as they realized they didn't have to keep up the pretense.

Six of the 36 of the originally gynephilic identified transwomen reported a shift to bisexuality and androphilia. This sort of shift has been widely reported before. Of course, these shifts are generally recognized to be a result of interpersonal autogynephilia,

"Autogynephilic MtF transsexual persons often report the fantasy of sexual intercourse as a woman with a man, that was repeatedly described as faceless and abstract. Yet this pseudoandrophilia has to be distinguished from genuine androphilia or homosexuality in MtF, or as Blanchard points it: "the effective erotic stimulus, however, is not the male physique per se, as it is in true homosexual attraction, but rather the thought of being a female, which is symbolized in the fantasy of being penetrated by a male. For these persons, the imagined — occasionally real — male sexual partner serves the same function as women's apparel or makeup, namely, to aid and intensify the fantasy of being a woman". Similarly, one of our participants that formally reported a change of sexual orientation from gynephilia towards androphilia stressed that "I always wanted to experience sexual intercourse as a woman but I did not know what to do with my male body before the hormone treatment. I hated male bodies in general before". In this case a reported change in sexual orientation from gynephilic to androphilic can be attributed

to autogynephilic fantasies."

The more interesting data in this study is all about the FtM transmen, about which we have far fewer studies. Of six originally androphilic FtMs, four of them experience a shift to being gynephilic during transition… and of the 33 originally gynephilic six experience a shift to being androphilic or bisexual.

> *"In gynephilic FtM a reported change of sexual orientation was less frequent. Six gynephilic FtM reported a change of sexual orientation towards bisexuality and androphilia in the present study. This may in part be explained by the fact that androphilic sexual behavior is complicated for FtM. Sex with male partners can induce intense gender dysphoria by being penetrated as a woman although feeling as a man. One participant in the study of Rowniak and Chesla stated that he didn't like being "feminized in bed" and others used the description that they were unable to have sex with men "until they were a man". Thus in these 6 participants androphilia may have been the original sexual orientation that became possible only after transitioning. In this case we wouldn't expect a genuine change of sexual orientation in these gynephilic FtM transsexual persons."*

I was friends with an FtM who stated exactly the same thing… that he 'identified' as and participated in the lesbian community because lesbians would let him be "butch", but straight men wouldn't. As a gay identified FtM, he could finally be both butch and express his native androphilia. He was in fact, autoandrophilic.

It is gratifying that the authors recognize the weaknesses of their study and make some recommendations for future studies,

> *"Self-reported sexual orientation studies have further been reported to be interfered by the fact that some persons do not answer the question truthfully. Some transsexual people for example may want to present themselves as particular feminine (MtF) or masculine (FtM) and thus "classical" transsexual persons. Participants in the present study might have biased their reports on purpose or unwittingly towards a more gender-typical presentation [w/ repect to target sex]. This may also involve worries on denial of sex reassignment surgery. We feel that attempts to minimize such worries are important in future studies. We also suggest that researchers should explicitly ask for autogynephilic and autoandrophilic sexual orientation."*

The fact that therapists and clinicians had not been making it clear that they knew that there were two types allowed transsexuals and the public to conflate the two types for several decades.

However with the publication of Blanchard's papers and subsequent dialog that occurred in the autogynephilic led community, notably by Anne Lawrence in the late '90s, a growing sense of unease spread as it became clear to many that the unitary conflation of the two types and the feminine essence and gender identity narratives wasn't being accepted by everyone.

While transsexual lying may have been necessary initially on the personal level for non-autogynephilic transsexuals to obtain the treatment they needed and were entitled to, this is no longer true. Instead, the singular personal lie has become a social lie, required by autogynephilic transsexuals to maintain the public facade they require to be "real", but at the expense of those whose lives they are attempting to mimic. Up to this point, the colonization of homosexual transsexual narratives by autogynephilic transsexuals had been a passive process, largely the result of autogynephilic transsexuals simply trying to get what they felt that they personally needed, as individuals. But with the publication of Bailey's *The Man Who Would Be Queen* in 2003, a new chapter was opened when leaders of the autogynephilic transsexual community organized to harass the author who wrote the simple truth in unflattering terms. (And just may organize to oppose this book too.) From this point the redefinition of the homosexual transsexual became an active process as the autogynephilic transsexual community perceived that the existence and contrast of homosexual transsexuals compared to autogynephilic transsexuals called into question their own true motivation to seek somatic feminization. On the one hand, they supported early transition for feminine boys who clearly would fit in better as girls, but with the rationalization that they too would have done so had the "proper support systems" been in place, or had they known that such transition was possible. Of course, the existence of an older homosexual transsexual population that had transitioned as teenagers in the so called "dark ages" before the internet, who now were deep stealth, occasionally became an embarrassment, but, given the natural reluctance for them to out themselves, didn't come out in sufficient numbers to upset the public relations spin of the autogynephilic transsexual community.

Bailey's book created emotional upset and denial of the two type typology among autogynephilic transsexuals as Alice Dreger in her wonderful book *Galileo's Middle Finger* explains,

> *"To understand the vehemence of the backlash against Bailey's book, you have to understand one more thing. There's a critical difference between autogynephilia and most other sexual orientations; Most other orientations aren't erotically disrupted simply by being labeled. When you call a typical*

gay man homosexual, you're not disturbing his sexual hopes and desires. By contrast, autogynephilia is perhaps best understood as a love that would really rather we didn't speak its name. The ultimate eroticism of autogynephilia lies in the idea of really becoming or being a woman, not in being a natal male who desires to be a woman. ... The erotic fantasy is to really be a woman. Indeed, according to a vision of transsexualism common among those transitioning from lives as privileged straight men to trans women, sex reassignment procedures are restorative rather than transformative... For Bailey or anyone else to call someone with armour de soi en femme an autogynephile or even a transgender woman — rather than simply a woman — is at some level to interfere with her core sexual desire. Such naming also risks questioning her core self-identity ... When they felt that Bailey was fundamentally threatening their selves and their social identities as women — well, it's because he was. That's what talking openly about autogynephilia necessarily does."

Consequences

A few years back, in an email, a knowledgeable sexologist I respect still managed to astound me by stating that the two types of transsexual didn't need to be differentiated and treated separately. Nothing could be further from the truth.

It should be obvious by now that prescribing puberty blockers, much less cross-sex hormones to autogynephilic teenagers does not make sense as their gender dysphoria has not yet solidified or even been expressed.

In transsexual support groups, homosexual transsexuals are in a minority position from the beginning. It is human nature to seek out those like themselves, so occasionally a homosexual transsexual finds a support group, but soon feels out-of-place and uncomfortable, unable to relate to autogynephiles and the issues that autogynephiles most want to discuss. Unless the support group is moderated by an experienced therapist, the naturally more masculine and dominant autogynephiles, accustomed to male privilege, will tend to monopolize the conversations. Further, most autogynephiles are strongly attracted to other transsexuals, especially to those who are physically and behaviorally more feminine, the homosexual transsexual minority may be subject to unwanted sexual advances from the autogynephilic majority. Naturally, finding no real support for, or mirroring of, her own concerns, and made uncomfortable by sexual objectification, the lone homosexual transsexual will quickly drift away, leaving the support group to the autogynephiles.

One of the most serious negative consequences of combining the two types of MTF transgender/transsexuals is that of sexual objectification and harassment. Autogynephiles are also gynandromorphophilic. That is, they experience a specific sexual attraction to transsexual people, especially those who are pre-op, young, and naturally feminine in appearance and behavior, to wit, young homosexual transsexuals in transition. This sexual attraction actually exceeds their attraction to women. Imagine the consequences of encouraging open and explicit discussions of sex and gender experiences in a group of comparatively masculine individuals used to lifelong male privilege while including young, naive, feminine individuals who are their most desirable sexual and romantic potential partners; But who do not as a general rule welcome such attention from autogynephiles.

S. Alejandra Velasquez writing for the transkids.us website noted,

> *"Teen hsts should not be required to attend support groups for older transsexuals. The two groups have nothing in common and many of us have had upsetting experiences being forced to attend meetings with people who have had a transvestic etiology as opposed to a homosexual one."*

In private dialogs with homosexual transsexuals, it is common to hear complaints about inappropriately prurient questions and comments from autogynephiles under the rubric of, "Oh, you can tell us! We're all girls here!"

A less obvious, but potentially counterproductive consequence of mixing the two types in therapy and support groups is that the two types will compare and contrast their own experiences and motivations to negative effect. For the autogynephilic type, they will be confronted with clear evidence that they do not live up to their idealization of "transsexuality" and femininity. Under such circumstances, envy and jealousy often arise, disrupting the goals of therapy. For the homosexual type, having been incorrectly informed that they are meeting with their peers, may look upon the, by stark contrast, masculine (in both appearance and behavior) autogynephilic transsexuals and create a falsely negative and confusing impression of themselves. For both groups, the confusion caused by discussing essentially incompatible histories and goals will disrupt any hoped for process. In fact, anger and resentment on both sides may arise, as one group tries to deny obvious autogynephilic motivations and natural gender typicality, attempt to mimic the other's history of gender atypicality and the other is required to pretend that their experiences are comparable lest they be seen as less than supportive, potentially invoking angry, spiteful responses. One group will express their grief and anger about having been ill-treated growing up for being naturally gender atypical, but expound on how transition has helped them be better accepted by society, while the other group complains that previously they held positions of respect but they now find that a transphobic society treats them worse for having attempted to live as women, but fail to pass.

Even having separated the two groups, a common problem encountered by both types is that of muddled conflation of the two group's experiences and goals:

The problems of homosexual transsexuals of both natal sexes are primarily social, not personal; they transition to improve their social status, as gender atypical individuals often experience discrimination and social exclusion. If anything, the most common personal issue is that of grieving, loneliness, and isolation from disapproving family. These are young people who have been obviously gender atypical since birth. This may mean that their family is disapproving and may have even disowned their child. They are not exploring their inner sense of "gender identity", which implicitly matched their gender atypical behavior since early childhood. They are living with the consequences of their long history of outward gender atypical presentation and sexual orientation. When they decide to "transition" it is not a big decision or change. It usually involves very little disruption to their lives, save for some potential additional disapproval from family or church; contrarily, most experience a social blossoming.

Because many homosexual transsexual youth experience familial rejection to become homeless, they are a very high risk of self-harming behaviors running from self-sabotage, substance abuse, risky sexual behaviors, cutting, to suicidal ideation and attempted suicide. These youths need social support services but in many localities, the fact that they are transsexual works against them as they are often placed in wrong sex segregated group homes or unsupportive foster families. Social workers may have a very poor understanding of the needs of gender atypical youth and feel uncomfortable working with them. The caring health worker should be aware of these difficulties and provide educational materials and advocate for their clients.

As with all health issues, prevention is better than cure. Health care providers are in a unique position to offer help to families with gender atypical children and teens understand and support these youth before relations deteriorate.

The problems of autogynephilic and autoandrophilic transsexuals on the other hand are primarily personal, not social... at least before transition. Most have very successful social lives, careers, marriages, family relationships. They are exploring their shifting inner sense of "gender identity" as they face the incongruity of their outwardly socially successful integration as one sex with their inner and usually secret desire to be the other sex. They are at war with themselves, as they deal with the guilt and shame, the dissonance of being socially successful as one sex, while always, in their inner sex life, obligatorily the other. When they decide to "transition" it really is a big decision and even bigger life change; most experience severe family and often career disruption, along with a sudden introduction to the social stigma of being notably gender atypical, in both behavior and appearance, in their new nominal gender role, unable to pass.

Gender therapists often conflate the two groups, making the common mistake that autogynephilic and autoandrophilic transsexuals are dealing with their gender atypicality, failing to recognize their autogynephilia or autoandrophilia, while simultaneously mistaking the homosexual group as dealing with conflicted inner gender identity. For example, suggesting to a homosexual transsexual that she perform some female gender affirming act in the privacy of her home will only be met with either confusion or derision, as her issues are social, not personal. Suggesting that a member of one group read the autobiographies of the other is less than helpful, for the same reason that combining the two groups for support is a bad idea.

Another mistake that gender therapists make is in regard to the heterosexual female partners, parents, siblings, and children of autogynephilic MTF transgender people when they, in effect by proxy, insist that these women and other family members accept the edited gender histories of their clients. A common behavior of autogynephilic transwomen in transition is to 'retcon', edit, their recollections and understanding of their sexual and gendered history to seem more "classically transsexual", more like the homosexual type in their childhood gender atypicality, denying their actual history of having been conventionally gender typical but secretly autogynephilically motivated. They may outright deny autogynephilic sexual arousal to cross-dressing, which may have been witnessed by parents and/or wives. Therapists, in their laudable goal of helping their clients accept themselves as they transition, having conflated the two types, may fail to recognize the extent of their clients' historical distortions. Or, if aware of them, fail to stress that while these edited idealizations of their client's history may be comforting to their clients, they are emotionally abusive to their client's wives and sometimes their parents. Further, in the long run, this edited history and denial of autogynephilia sets up their clients for an emotional crisis when that denial mechanism fails, perhaps with even fatal results.

Clinicians involved in family therapy where one partner is autogynephilic or autoandrophilic will often find themselves in an invidious position as the non-trans individual experiences severe loss and grief that must be acknowledged while the transsexual individual expects their partner to be supportive, happy, and even celebratory during their transition process.

The obvious mismatch between expectations, needs, and the ability to meet those needs lead to acrimony. Additionally, many non-trans individuals involved find the social, sartorial, and somatic changes in their partner to be sexually repulsive. The unhappy statistical truth is that such relationships are far more likely to end than to find a resolution that allows the intimate relationship to continue. Interviews with ex-spouses often point out that they felt that clinicians failed to be supportive of their needs and put those of the transitioning spouse above theirs. The wise clinician will avoid these situations as there is rarely any way to resolve both spouses' needs within the relationship. The best that can be accomplished is to lay the groundwork for mutual respect for each in a post separation / divorce relationship. This last is especially important if there are children involved.

Finally, it is important to know that autogynephilic MTF transsexuals are at elevated risk of co-morbid mental health issues, from severe anxiety to deep depression. With greater understanding compassion for the true nature of both types of transsexual / transgender people, we should see better long-term results from therapy.

Separating the two types isn't just important during therapy. Under no circumstance should a young homosexual transsexual be required to share a hospital room with an older adult autogynephilic transsexual. The hospital administration usually has no real clue about the realities of transsexuality and transsexuals, and think that we are all the same. No one would think of asking a young lady to share a hospital room with an older straight man… but that is in effect what is happening in hospitals on a regular basis. Autogynephilic transsexuals are sexually attracted to women, and often, even especially, to young MTF homosexual transsexuals. Further, a fair number of autogynephilic individuals sexualize the very act, the process of changing sex, both in themselves and in others. Due to a lifetime of socialization as men, and only limited experience in their new gender role, these individuals often do not recognize appropriate boundaries. Homosexual transsexuals should not be so exposed when they are at their most physically and emotionally vulnerable point in their young lives!

I myself had a very upsetting incident when I had SRS when I shared a room with a stranger, an autogynephilic transsexual, who clearly did not respect nor even understand appropriate boundaries that woman observe with other women, much less avoiding behaving in a pruriently inappropriate yet simultaneously jealous and hostile manner.

17 HOW TO TELL THEM APART

In his 2003 book, *The Man Who Would Be Queen*, J. Michael Bailey included a quiz. As an homage, I rewrote the quiz, to tighten up the criteria, more accurately weighted the items, and expanded it based on what science has learned about the two types. I also coupled the items with equally weighted items that would differentiate homosexual from autogynephilic transwomen. As with Bailey's original quiz, it is meant more an educational than an actual diagnostic tool:

Autogynephilic vs. Homosexual Transsexual Quiz:

Start at Zero. Ask each question, and if the answer is "Yes," add or subtract the number as indicated by the sign (+ or -) next to each question. (Substitute the value in parentheses when applicable.)

+15 Have you worn women's clothing in private and, during at least three of those times, become so sexually aroused that you masturbated? {If you answered yes: STOP! This one is definitional, you are autogynephilic.}

-15 Have you been sexually active with a man (only a man, never had sexual intercourse with a woman, and more than ten times with a man) while pre-op and carefully avoided using or letting your partner touch your genitals (allowed no more than three times)?

+3 Have you been married to a woman? (Add +5 if married more than once.)

–3 Is your ideal partner a straight man? (Add -5 if married to a straight man.)

+3 Whether married or not, have you sired a child? (Add +5 if more than one.)

−3 Whether married (to a straight man) or not, while living as a woman have you adopted or foster-mothered a child? (Add -5 if more than one.) {Note: You must have initiated the process while living as woman, not a carry-over from a pre-transition family, nor step-children by a female partner.}

+5 Are you nearly as attracted to women as to men? Or more attracted to women? Or equally uninterested in both, or unsure?

-5 Does this describe you? "I find the idea of having sex with men very sexually exciting, but the idea of having sex with women is not at all appealing."

+1 As a child, did people think you were about as masculine as other boys?

-1 As a child, did people think you were an unusually feminine boy?

+1 Were you over the age of 30 when you began to live full-time as a woman? (+5 if over age 40)

−1 Were you under the age of 25 when you began to live full-time as a woman? (-5 if under age 20)

+3 While living as a man, have you ever been in the military or worked as a policeman, truck driver, construction worker, or been a computer programmer, businessman, lawyer, scientist, professor, engineer, or physician, or other male dominated industry position?

-3 Have you worked as a child-care worker (not just a casual or convenient baby-sitter), hair stylist, beautician (other than electrologist), lingerie model, secretary, nurse, or other pink-collar job?

+5 Did you grow out and wear facial hair (mustache, side-burns, beard, etc.) at any time in your life?

-5 Did you begin puberty blockers or HRT soon enough to avoid the need for electrolysis?

Finally, if the person has been on hormones for at least six months, ask yourself this question:

If you didn't already know that this person was a transsexual, would you still have suspected that she was not a natural-born woman?

+1 if your answer is "Yes" (if you would have suspected)

-1 If your answer is "No".

If the sum is greater than zero, the person is likely an autogynephilic transsexual. If the sum is less than zero, the person is likely a homosexual transsexual. The larger the absolute value, the higher the confidence in the result. The scale range is +50 to -50.

BIBLIOGRAPHY

This is a selected bibliography of references from *On the Science of Changing Sex*. These are the papers and books that I feel are the most important for those who wish to come up to a minimal level of literacy on the science that conclusively tests the two type taxonomy hypothesis. Be cautious of reading only the abstracts of papers behind paywalls. The abstract may not completely or even accurately describe the data or its import in supporting or refuting a given hypothesis.

Transgender:

Benjamin Cerf Harris, "Likely Transgender Individuals in U.S. Federal Administrative Records and the 2010 Census"
http://www.census.gov/srd/carra/15_03_Likely_Transgender_Individuals _in_ARs_and_2010Cen sus.pdf

This study shows that there are only 90,000 transfolk who have socially transitioned in the United States out of 300 million people. This is important because when the public hears "transgender" they think "post-transition". Yet, in recent surveys, 1.4 million people "identify" as "transgender", which means that the public perception of who is "transgender" and who identifies as "transgender" is off by a factor of 15X.

Lindsay Collin, Sari L. Reisner Vin Tangpricha, and Michael Goodman, "Prevalence of Transgender Depends on the "Case" Definition: A Systematic Review" (2016) Journal of Sexual Medicine
http://doi.org/10.1016/j.jsxm.2016.02.001

Speaking of incidence rates, there is a correlation between the percentage of the two types of transsexuals transitioning and a culture's level of individualism. The "AngloSphere", (e.g. United States, Canada, U.K.

Australia, etc.) is one of the most individualist culture in the world and has the greatest percentage of gynephilic/autogynephilic transwomen.

Anne A. Lawrence (2010), "Societal Individualism Predicts Prevalence of Nonhomosexual Orientation in Male-to-Female Transsexualism" http://www.springerlink.com/content/x556338354658m3w/

Anne A. Lawrence (2013), "More Evidence that Societal Individualism Predicts Prevalence of Nonhomosexual Orientation in Male-to-Female Transsexualism" http://link.springer.com/article/10.1007/s10508-013-0083-3#page-1

Two Type Taxonomy

For an excellent overview on the taxonomy, objections, and critique of those objections one may start with Anne Lawrence:

Lawrence, A., "Autogynephilia and the Typology of Male-to-Female Transsexualism: Concepts and Controversies", European Psychologist, 22, 39-54. (2017) http://www.annelawrence.com/autogynephilia_&_MtF_typology.html

Norman Fisk, M.D. wrote this next paper that changed the way that the medical community treated Male-To-Female (MTF) transsexuality. Previously, in recognition that there were in fact two types of transsexuals / transgender, one that was autogynephilic, in the same etiological taxon as transvestites and one that was exclusively androphilic and appeared to be in the same etiological taxon as feminine gay men, the clinicians attempted to "gate-keep" the autogynephilic type from receiving services, leading to extensive misrepresentations by the autogynephilic type that continues today. This paper proposed that they should both be treated similarly under the new unitary diagnosis of "gender dysphoria", not as a replacement for the taxonomy, but in recognition that both types were equally in need of palliative medical interventions:

Fisk, N., "Editorial: Gender dysphoria syndrome–the conceptualization that liberalizes indications for total gender reorientation and implies a broadly based multi-dimensional rehabilitative regimen." (1974) Western Journal of Medicine https://www.ncbi.nlm.nih.gov/pmc/articles/PMC1130142/

These next papers have data that supports the Two Type Taxonomy of MTF transsexual and transgender, most importantly, data showing a very strong correlation between sexual orientation and autogynephilia in which putatively exclusively androphilic transwomen report significantly less autogynephilia than non-androphilic transwomen. They also show that age of social transition, childhood gender atypicality, physical appearance (passability), and brain structure & responses also correlate with the two types. These studies collectively involve over a thousand transsexuals.

Buhrich N, McConaghy N., "Two clinically discrete syndromes of transsexualism." British Journal of Psychiatry. 1978 Jul;133:73-6.

Two types of cross-gender identity. Freund K, Steiner BW, Chan S. Archives of Sexual Behavior. 1982 Feb;11(1):49-63.

Typology of male-to-female transsexualism. Blanchard, Ray. Archives of Sexual Behavior. Vol 14(3) Jun 1985, 247-261.

Heterosexual and homosexual gender dysphoria. Blanchard, Ray; Clemmensen, Leonard H; Steiner, Betty W. Archives of Sexual Behavior. Vol 16(2) Apr 1987, 139-152.

Nonhomosexual gender dysphoria. Blanchard, Ray. Journal of Sex Research. Vol 24 1988, 188-193.

 Blanchard, R., "The concept of autogynephilia and the typology of male gender dysphoria." Journal of Nervous & Mental Disease. Vol 177(10) Oct 1989, 616-623.

Blanchard, R., 'Nonmonotonic relation of autogynephilia and heterosexual attraction". J Abnorm Psychol. 1992 May;101(2):271-6.

Blanchard R., "Varieties of autogynephilia and their relationship to gender dysphoria." Arch Sex Behav. 1993 Jun;22(3):241-51.

Blanchard, Ray, "Clinical observations and systematic studies of autogynephilia". Journal of Sex & Marital Therapy. Vol 17(4) Win 1991, 235-251.

C. D. Doorn, J. Poortinga and A. M. Verschoor, "Cross-gender identity in transvestites and male transsexuals"
http://www.springerlink.com/content/u63p723776v57m11/

Smith Yolanda L. S.; Van Goozen Stephanie H. M.; Kuiper A. J.; Cohen-Kettenis Peggy T., "Transsexual subtypes : Clinical and theoretical significance", Psychiatry research (Psychiatry res.) 2005, vol. 137, no3, pp. 151-160

Sex Reassignment : Predictors and Outcomes Of Treatment for Transsexuals / Yolanda Louise Susanne Smith – [S.l.] : [s.n.], 2002 – Tekst. – Proefschrift Universiteit Utrecht
https://dspace.library.uu.nl/bitstream/handle/1874/429/inhoud.htm?sequence=15

Anne A. Lawrence, "Sexuality Before and After Male-to-Female Sex Reassignment Surgery" 2005
http://link.springer.com/article/10.1007/s10508-005-1793-y

Nuttbrock, et al., "A Further Assessment of Blanchard's Typology of Homosexual versus Non-Homosexual or Autogynephilic Gender Dysphoria", Archives of Sexual Behavior
http://www.springerlink.com/content/b48tkl425217331j/

Laube et al., "Sexual Behavior, Desire, and Psychosexual Experience in Gynephilic and Androphilic Trans Women: A Cross-Sectional Multicenter Study" March 2020 Journal of Sexual Medicine
https://www.researchgate.net/publication/339738869_Sexual_Behavior_D esire_and_Psychosex ual_Experience_in_Gynephilic_and_Androphilic_Trans_Women_A_Cross -Sectional_Multicente r_Study

Sadr, M., Khorashad, B.S., Talaei, A. et al. "2D:4D Suggests a Role of Prenatal Testosterone in Gender Dysphoria" Archives of Sexual Behavior (2020) https://doi.org/10.1007/s10508-020-01630-0

Clinicians have long noted differences in physical appearance of the two types in which the exclusively androphilic transwomen were significantly better at passing. In one study in Canada, differences in height and body size were noted, but a study in the Netherlands failed to replicate this effect. But when they evaluated physical appearance there was a significant effect:

Ray Blanchard, Robert Dickey, Corey L. Jones, "Comparison of Height and Weight in Homosexual Versus Nonhomosexual Male Gender Dysphorics" http://www.springerlink.com/content/w318411nq4q7387u/

Lawrence, A., "Male-to-female transsexual subtypes: Sexual arousal with cross-dressing and physical measurements"

Yolanda L.S. Smith, Stephanie H.M. van Goozen, A.J. Kuiper, Peggy T. Cohen-Kettenis, "Transsexual subtypes: Clinical and theoretical significance"

Tim C. van de Grift, Peggy T. Cohen-Kettenis, Thomas D. Steensma, Griet De Cuypere, Hertha Richter-Appelt, Ira R. H. Haraldsen, Rieky E. G. Dikmans, Susanne C. Cerwenka, , Baudewijntje P. C. Kreukels, "Body Satisfaction and Physical Appearance in Gender Dysphoria" Archives of Sexual Behavior DOI: 10.1007/s10508-015-0614-1

Research into perceived shifts of sexual orientation in transsexuals has revealed an important feature of the life arcs of non-exclusively androphilic transwomen which causes confusion and 'noise' in some studies when the researchers aren't careful to sort on their primary (original) sexual orientation. Non-exclusively androphilic transwomen often report that their sexual orientation shifted from primarily gynephilic to bisexual or even "exclusively" androphilic during social transition or soon after SRS.

However, research strongly suggests that this in effect of interpersonal autogynephilic ideation:

Daskalos CT., "Changes in the sexual orientation of six heterosexual male-to-female transsexuals."
http://www.springerlink.com/content/pu44808u15q78k21/

Anne Lawrence, "Letter to the Editor" (in response to Daskalos)
http://link.springer.com/content/pdf/10.1023%2FA%3A1018725518592

Matthias K. Auer, Johannes Fuss, Nina Hohne, Gunter K. Stalla, Caroline Sievers, "Transgender Transitioning and Change of Self-Reported Sexual Orientation"
http://www.plosone.org/article/fetchObject.action?uri=info%3Adoi%2F1 0.1371%2Fjournal.pone. 0110016&representation=PDF

Anne A. Lawrence, "Sexuality Before and After Male-to-Female Sex Reassignment Surgery" 2005
http://link.springer.com/article/10.1007/s10508-005-1793-y

Research on Transsexual Brains shows very strong support for the two type taxonomy in that exclusively androphilic transwomen and exclusively gynephilic transmen show shifts in sexually dimorphic brain structures and responses toward the opposite sex (toward their gender identity) BEFORE Hormone Replacement Therapy (HRT) while non-exclusively-androphilic transwomen do not. It's important to know that HRT causes such shifts and thus studies with subjects on HRT do not offer insight into the etiology of either type.

Guillamon, A et al., "A Review of the Status of Brain Structure Research in Transsexualism" Arch Sex Behav (2016). doi:10.1007/s10508-016-0768-5

Spizzirri, G., et al., "Grey and white matter volumes either in treatment-naïve or hormone-treated transgender women: a voxel-based morphometry study" Nature Scientific Reports (2018). DOI:10.1038/s41598-017-17563-z

Dörner G, Rohde W, Schott G, Schnabl C., "On the LH response to oestrogen and LH-RH in transsexual men." Experimental Clinical Endrocrinology (1983) http://www.ncbi.nlm.nih.gov/pubmed/6317420

Dörner G., "Neuroendocrine response to estrogen and brain differentiation in heterosexuals, homosexuals, and transsexuals." Archives of Sexual Behavior (1988)
http://www.ncbi.nlm.nih.gov/pubmed/3282489?dopt=Abstract

Dörner G, Rohde W, Seidel K, Haas W, Schott GS."On the evocability of a positive oestrogen feedback action on LH secretion in transsexual men and

women." Endokrinology (1976)
http://www.ncbi.nlm.nih.gov/pubmed/1244197

Ivanka Savic, Stefan Arver, "Sex Dimorphism of the Brain in Male-to-Female Transsexuals"
http://cercor.oxfordjournals.org/content/early/2011/04/05/cercor.bhr032

Lajos Simon, Lajos R. Kozák, Viktória Simon, Pál Czobor, Zsolt Unoka, Ádám Szabó, Gábor Csukly, "Regional Grey Matter Structure Differences between Transsexuals and Healthy Controls—A Voxel Based Morphometry Study" 10.1371/journal.pone.0083947

Eileen Luders, et al., "Increased Cortical Thickness in Male-to-Female Transsexualism" Journal of Behavioral and Brain Science, July 2011
http://dbm.neuro.uni-jena.de/pdf-files/Luders-JBBS11.pdf

Leire Zubiaurre-Elorza et al, "Cortical Thickness in Untreated Transsexuals" Cerebral Cortex, August 2012
http://cercor.oxfordjournals.org/content/early/2012/08/30/cercor.bhs267.abstract

 Hulshoff Pol, H. E., Cohen-Kettenis, P. T., Van Haren, N. E., Peper, J. S., Brans, R. G., Cahn, W., et al. (2006). "Changing your sex changes your brain: Influences of testosterone and estrogen on adult human brain structure." European Journal of Endocrinology, 155(Suppl. 1), S107-S114.
http://eje-online.org/cgi/content/full/155/suppl_1/S107

Garcia-Falgueras A, Swaab DF. "A sex difference in the hypothalamic uncinate nucleus: relationship to gender identity." Brain. 2008
http://brain.oxfordjournals.org/cgi/reprint/131/12/3132

Brain Sexual Dimorphism

Liu, et Al.,"Integrative structural, functional, and transcriptomic analyses of sex-biased brain organization in humans", PNAS (2020)
https://doi.org/10.1073/pnas.1919091117

Autism

Clinicians have been noting that transfolk are more likely to be autistic than the general population, especially Female-to-Male (FtM) transmen. Interestingly, there is a difference in the autism-like behaviors between androphilic and gynephilic transwomen in which androphilic are identical to women and gynephilic identical to men.

Jones, et Al, "Female-To-Male Transsexual People and Autistic Traits", J. Autism Dev. Discord. DOI: 10.1007/s10803-011-1227-8

Pasterski, et al., "Traits of Autism Spectrum Disorders in Adults with Gender Dysphoria", Archives of Sexual Behavior (2013) https://doi.org/10.1007/s10508-013-0154-5

Shumer et al., "Evaluation of Asperger Syndrome in Youth Presenting to a Gender Dysphoria Clinic", LGBT Health (2016) https://doi.org/10.1089/lgbt.2015.0070

van der Meisen, et al., "Prevalence of the Wish to be the Opposite Gender in Adolescents and Adults with Autism Spectrum Disorder", Archives of Sexual Behavior (2018) https://doi.org/10.1007/s10508-018-1218-3

"Avoidant Sexuality"

Several clinicians have noted that there is a difference between exclusively androphilic transwomen and gynephilic transwomen in their sexual interaction with others. These papers explore the correlation between being "avoidant", that is, avoid the use of their pre-op genitalia, and sexual orientation / age of gender dysphoria onset.

S. Cerwenka, et al., "Sexual Behavior of Gender Dysphoric Individuals Before Gender-Confirming Interventions: A European Multicenter Study" (2014)

"Clinical Patterns Among Male Transsexual Candidates with Erotic Interest in Males" Frank Leavitt, Ph.D., Jack C. Berger, M.D. http://www.springerlink.com/content/fp15j71n57474k11/

There is one paper that attempted to statistically test whether the two type topology was in fact taxonic. The paper had serious methodological problems due to failure to properly sort truly exclusively androphilic transwomen from those who were in fact originally gynephilic but had experienced a perceived shift in sexual orientation. Autogynephilic and Even More Autogynephilic

Jaimie F. Veale, "Evidence Against a Typology: A Taxometric Analysis of the Sexuality of Male-to-Female Transsexuals" Archives Sexual Behavior DOI 10.1007/s10508-014-0275-5

Anne A. Lawrence, "Veale's (2014) Critique of Blanchard's Typology Was Invalid" Archive Sexual Behavior DOI 10.1007/s10508-014-0383-2

Homosexual Transsexuals

Papers on the Fraternal Birth Order Effect in androphilic males, both conventional gay men and transwomen strongly support the two type taxonomy and potentially an effect that differentiates androphilic transwomen from masculine gay men. Exclusively androphilic transwomen, as a population, have more older brothers than non-exclusively-androphilic (gynephilic) transwomen and men in the general population. While gay men also show this same effect, it is NOT as strong as it is in androphilic transwomen.

Blanchard, R., "Fraternal Birth Order, Family Size, and Male Homosexuality: Meta-Analysis of Studies Spanning 25 Years", Archives of Sexual Behavior, (2017), https://link.springer.com/article/10.1007/s10508-017-1007-4

Blanchard, R., & Sheridan, P. M. (1992). "Sibship size, sibling sex ratio, birth order, and parental age in homosexual and nonhomosexual gender dysphorics." Journal of Nervous and Mental Diseases, 180, 40–47.

Blanchard, Bogaert, "Homosexuality in men and number of older brothers"

http://ajp.psychiatryonline.org/cgi/content/abstract/153/1/27?ijkey=e18 6877631aa1c47de8fd859 310668c21bcd25ef&keytype2=tf_ipsecsha

Anthony F. Bogaert, "Biological versus nonbiological older brothers and men's sexual orientation"
http://www.pnas.org/content/103/28/10771.full

Green, R. (2000). "Birth order and ratio of brothers to sisters in transsexuals. Psychological Medicine", 30, 789–795.

Blanchard, R., Zucker, K., Cohen-Kettenis, P., Gooren, L., & Bailey, J. (1996). "Birth order and sibling sex ratio in two samples of Dutch gender-dysphoric homosexual males." Archives of Sexual Behavior, 25, 495–514.

Poasa, K. H., Blanchard, R., Zucker, K. J. (2004). "Birth order in transgendered males from Polynesia: A quantitative study of Samoan fa'afafine." Journal of Sex and Marital Therapy, 30, 13–23.

Bogeart, et al, "Male homosexuality and maternal immune responsivity to the Y-linked protein NLGN4Y" (2018)
https://doi.org/10.1073/pnas.1705895114

Weinrich, et al., "Effects of recalled childhood gender nonconformity on adult genitoerotic role and AIDS exposure" Archives of Sexual Behavior, 1992) https://link.springer.com/article/10.1007/BF01542256

Moskowitz, et al., "The Influence of Physical Body Traits and Masculinity on Anal Sex Roles in Gay and Bisexual Men", Archives of Sexual Behavior, (2011) https://link.springer.com/article/10.1007/s10508-011-9754-0

Wampold, C., "The Association Between Fraternal Birth Order and Anal-Erotic Roles of Men Who Have Sex with Men", Archives of Sexual Behavior, (2018) https://link.springer.com/article/10.1007/s10508-018-1237-0

Swift-Gallant, A. et al., "Gender Nonconformity and Birth Order in Relation to Anal Sex Role Among Gay Men" Archives of Sexual Behavior (2018) https://doi.org/10.1007/s10508-017-0980-y

Cross cultural aspects of androphilic transgender behavior and identity:

Bailey, et al., "Sexual Orientation, Controversy, and Science", Psychological Science in the Public Interest, doi: 10.1177/1529100616637616

Vanderlaan, et al., "Elevated Kin-Directed Altruism Emerges in Childhood and Is Linked to Feminine Gender Expression in Samoan Fa'afafine: A Retrospective Study" Archives of Sexual Behavior DOI: 10.1007/s10508-016-0884-2

Vasey, P. et al., "What can the Samoan Fa'afafine Teach Us About the Western Concept of Gender Identity Disorder in Childhood?", (2007) Perspectives on Biology and Medicine, http://muse.jhu.edu/article/222247

Vasey, P. "The Evolution of Male Androphilia" Personal Website: http://people.uleth.ca/~paul.vasey/PLV/Evolution_Androphilia.html

Petterson, L. "Male Bisexuality In Samoa" (2012) University of Lethbridge Thesis https://www.uleth.ca/dspace/bitstream/handle/10133/3745/PETTERSON_LANNA_MSC2015_T HESIS.pdf

Autogynephilia

Anne Lawrence, M.D. solicited material from autogynephilic transwomen and performed an analysis of its content. Her book, ironically entitled *Men Trapped in Men's Bodies – Naratives of Autogynephilic Transsexualism* is the result. It is an absolute must read for anyone who sincerely wishes to understand how autogynephilia is experienced in non-exclusively-androphilic transwomen.

Dr. Lawrence has published other papers on autogynephilia which are also must reads:

"Autogynephilia: A paraphilic model of gender identity disorder." Lawrence A. Journal of Gay and Lesbian Psychotherapy. 2004 Vol. 8 Numbers 1/2. http://www.annelawrence.com/autogynephilia,_a_paraphilic_model_of_GID.pdf

"Becoming What We Love: Autogynephilic Transsexualism Conceptualized as an Expression of Romantic Love", Lawrence A. http://www.annelawrence.com/becoming_what_we_love.pdf

Papers on Autogynephilia in the general population:

Langstrom, et al., "Transvestic Fetishism in the General Population" Journal of Sex & Marital Therapy, (2011) http://dx.doi.org/10.1080/00926230590477934

Baur, E., et Al, "Paraphilic Sexual Interests & Sexually Coersive Behavior: A Population-Based Twin Study" Archives of Sexual Behavior: DOI:10.1007/s10508-015-0674-2

Kevin J. Hsu, A. M. Rosenthal, J. Michael Bailey, "The Psychometric Structure of Items Assessing Autogynephilia"

Archives of Sexual Behavior, DOI 10.1007/s10508-014-0397-9

Papers on the correlation between autogynephilia and gynandromorphophilia:

K. J. Hsu, A. M. Rosenthal, D. I. Miller and J. M. Bailey, "Sexual Arousal Patterns of Autogynephilic Cross-dressing Men" https://www.researchgate.net/publication/308036975_Sexual_Arousal_Pat terns_of_Autogyneph ilic_Male_Cross-Dressers

K. J. Hsu, A. M. Rosenthal, D. I. Miller and J. M. Bailey, "Who are gynandromorphophilic men? Characterizing men with sexual interest in transgender women" http://d-miller.github.io/assets/HsuEtAl2015.pdf

Jaimie F. Veale, Dave E. Clarke and Terri C. Lomax, "Sexuality of Male-to-Female Transsexuals" http://www.springerlink.com/content/bp2235t8261q23u3/

Anne A. Lawrence and J. Michael Bailey Transsexual Groups in Veale et al. (2008) are "Autogynephilic" and "Even More Autogynephilic" http://www.springerlink.com/content/u473w370g11vx758/

Jaimie F. Veale, David E. Clarke and Terri C. Lomax Reply to Lawrence and Bailey (2008) http://www.springerlink.com/content/cm253l3m3148377/

Blanchard R, Collins PI., "Men with sexual interest in transvestites, transsexuals, and she-males" http://www.ncbi.nlm.nih.gov/pubmed/8245926

Blanchard R., "The she-male phenomenon and the concept of partial autogynephilia" http://www.informaworld.com/smpp/content~db=all~content=a789560 133 Sumia et al., "Current and recalled childhood gender identity in community youth in comparison to referred adolescents seeking sex reassignment", Journal of Adolescence http://www.sciencedirect.com/science/article/pii/S0140197117300155

Vrouenraets, L. et al. "Perceptions of Sex, Gender, and Puberty Suppression: A Qualitative Analysis of Transgender Youth" Archives of Sexual Behavior (2016). doi:10.1007/s10508-016-0764-9

Zucker KJ\, Wild J, Bradley SJ, Lowry CB., "Physical attractiveness of boys with gender identity

disorder." Archives of Sexual Behavior. 1993 Feb;22(1):23-36. http://link.springer.com/article/10.1007/BF01552910

Stephanie A. Mcdermid, Kenneth J. Zucker, Susan J. Bradley, Dianne M. Maing, "Effects of Physical Appearance on Masculine Trait Ratings of Boys and Girls with Gender Identity Disorder" Archives of Sexual Behavior http://link.springer.com/article/10.1023/A%3A1018650401386

Sari R. Fridell, Kenneth J. Zucker, Susan J. Bradley, Dianne M. Maing, "Physical attractiveness of girls with gender identity disorder" Archives of Sexual Behavior http://link.springer.com/article/10.1007/BF02437905

Kristina R. Olson, Aidan C. Key, Nicholas R. Eaton, "Gender Cognition in Transgender Children", Psychological Science

Thomas D. Steensma, Roeline Biemond, Fijgie de Boer and Peggy T. Cohen-Kettenis, "Desisting and persisting gender dysphoria after childhood: A qualitative follow-up study" http://ccp.sagepub.com/content/early/2011/01/06/1359104510378303

Sarah M. Burke, Willeke M. Menks, Peggy T. Cohen-Kettenis, Daniel T. Klink, Julie Bakker, "Click-Evoked Otoacoustic Emissions in Children and Adolescents with Gender Identity Disorder" Archives of Sexual Behavior, DOI 10.1007/s10508-014-0278-2

Gülgöz, S., Glazier, J. J., Enright, E. A., Alonso, D. J., Durwood, L. J., Fast, A. A., Lowe, R., Ji, C., Heer, J., Martin, C. M., & Olson, K. R. (2019). Similarity in Transgender and Cisgender Children's Gender Development. PNAS. doi: 10.1073/pnas.1909367116 Link to pdf

Olson, K.R., & Gülgöz, S. (2018). Early Findings from the TransYouth Project: Gender Development in Transgender Children. Child Development Perspectives, 12(2), 93-97. Link to pdf

Androphilia and Autoandrophilia in Transmen and Women

While not as well researched as the correlation between autogynephilia and gynephilia in transwomen and men, there is some regarding non-gynephilic transmen. Autoandrophilia occurs in 0.4% to 0.5% of women in the general population (compared to autogynephilia in 2.8% to 4.5% of men).

S. Colton Meier, Seth T. Pardo, Christine Labuski, Julia Babcock,

"Measures of Clinical Health among Female-to-Male Transgender Persons as a Function of Sexual Orientation"
http://link.springer.com/article/10.1007/s10508-012-0052-2

Walter Bockting, Autumn Benner and Eli Coleman, "Gay and Bisexual Identity Development

Among Female-to-Male Transsexuals in North America: Emergence of a Transgender Sexuality"
http://www.springerlink.com/content/775x6m1p0j045313/

Eli Coleman, Walter O. Bockting, and Louis Gooren, "Homosexual and bisexual identity in sex-reassigned female-to-male transsexuals"
http://link.springer.com/article/10.1007/BF01552911

Robert Diekey and Judith Stephens, "Female-to-male transsexualism, heterosexual type: Two cases"
http://link.springer.com/article/10.1007/BF01541857

Dorothy Clare and Bryan Tully, "Transhomosexuality, or the Dissociation of Orientation and Sex Object Choice"
http://link.springer.com/article/10.1007/BF01541679

Meredith L. Chivers and J. Michael Bailey, "Sexual Orientation of Female-to-Male Transsexuals: A Comparison of Homosexual and Nonhomosexual Types" http://link.springer.com/article/10.1023/A%3A1001915530479

Stefan Rowniak and Catherine Chesla, "Coming Out for a Third Time: Transmen, Sexual Orientation, and Identity"
http://link.springer.com/article/10.1007/s10508-012-0036-2

Robert J. Stoller, "Transvestism in Women"
http://www.springerlink.com/content/tj0lw18644n18g02/

Langstrom, et al., "Transvestic Fetishism in the General Population"
Journal of Sex & Marital Therapy, (2011)
http://dx.doi.org/10.1080/00926230590477934

Baur, E., et Al, "Paraphilic Sexual Interests & Sexually Coercive Behavior: A Population-Based Twin Study" Archives of Sexual Behavior:
DOI:10.1007/s10508-015-0674-2

ABOUT THE AUTHOR

"Kay Brown" is the pen name used by Candice H. Brown Elliott for writing about transsexual and transgender science, history, and politics. She was diagnosed as transsexual as a teenager in high school in 1975 by Dr. Norman Fisk, the man who coined the term, "gender dysphoria".

Candice was a founding member of the ACLU Transsexual Rights Committee in 1980 and has assiduously worked for better legal and social treatment of transsexuals all her life.

She has a dual degree in physics and psychology, minor in biology. Like many successful high tech Silicon Valley entrepreneurs, Candice dropped out of graduate school at Stanford University to work at start-up companies. She has been granted over one hundred US patents, published scientific & technical papers, articles, and a textbook chapter. She was awarded the Otto Schade Prize for her contributions in color flat panels displays.

Candice lives in the wine country north of San Francisco with her husband Jeff. She has two foster/adopted daughters both now grown. In semi-retirement she writes science fiction novels under the pen name "Seaby Brown" and is a commercial pilot & flight instructor at the local airport (CFI, CFII, MEI).

Candice writes and maintains essays On The Science of Changing Sex at sillyolme.wordpress.com